CROSSING *the* SAUER

CROSSING *the* SAUER

A *Memoir* OF
WORLD WAR II

CHARLES *Reis* FELIX

Burford Books

Epigraph reprinted with permission of Simon & Schuster from *Moments of Reprieve* by Primo Levi. Translated from the Italian by Ruth Feldman. English translation Copyright © 1986 by Simon & Schuster, Inc.

"Dinner for One Please James" Words and music by Michael Carr. © 1936, reproduced by permission of Peter Maurice Music Co Ltd, London WC2H 0QY.

"Dinner for One Please James" by Michael Carr. © Peter Maurice Music. All Rights administered by Chappell & Co. (ASCAP). All rights reserved. Used by permission. Warner Bros. Publications U.S. Inc., Miami FL 33014.

Printed in the United States of America.

10 9 8 7 6 5 4 3 2 1

Library of Congress Cataloging-in-Publication Data
Felix, Charles Reis.
    Crossing the Sauer : a memoir of World War II / Charles Reis Felix.
        p.   cm.
    ISBN 1-58080-099-8
        1. Felix, Charles Reis. 2. World War, 1939–1945—Personal narrative, American. 3. World War, 1939–1945—Campaigns—Germany. 4. United States. Army—Biography. I. Title.

D811.F436 A3 2002
940.54'8173—dc21
                                                        2002016480

FOR BARBARA

HOW TRUSTWORTHY can a memoir be when it is written some fifty-five years after the events in question have taken place? Primo Levi addresses that issue with his customary intelligence in the Preface to his *Moments of Reprieve*, which is, so to speak, a memoir of Auschwitz.

> *It is possible that the distance in time has accentuated the tendency to round out the facts or heighten the colors: this tendency, or temptation, is an integral part of writing, without it one does not write stories but rather accounts. Nevertheless, the episodes on which I have built each of these stories actually did take place, and the characters did exist, even if, for obvious reasons, I have often changed their names.*
>
> Primo Levi, *Moments of Reprieve*

Contents

Prologue

1 Fontainebleau 3

2 Berseglaria 14

3 The Artillery Replacements 25

4 The First Week .38

5 Crossing the Sauer 44

6 Jelich 68

7 Nobody Gets Out 74

8 *"Ich Spreche Deutsch ein Wenig"* 80

9 The Assault Platoon 84

10 Whitewash 93

11 Jelich and the Roll 96

12 Footsteps 101

13 The Luger 108

14 A Dirty Trick 112

15 Major Pusey 118

16 The Rear 132

17 Captain Baker 144

18 The Priest Protecting the Furniture 151

19 Commanders 159

20 Folenius 167

21 Frankfurt 179

22 Finis 183

Epilogue

I HEARD MY FAVORITE LINE of the war in France. A comely woman, definitely not a farmer's wife, came walking down the street accompanied by an attentive American officer. An old French woman, nodding in her direction, said to me, *"Elle zig-zig avec Boche."* Yes, I thought, *et maintenant elle zig-zig avec Américains. C'est la vie.*

I heard my second most memorable line in Germany. A German stood in the street and looked about his town. It had undergone a severe artillery shelling from both sides. It was in ruins. You had to make your way around piles of rubble. No building was left untouched. Some had only partial walls standing. Starved horses, their ribs showing, lay dead in the fields, victims of shrapnel, their legs straight up in the air, rigid. The German surveyed his town and said morosely to me, *"Krieg nicht gut."* Good, I thought. I'm glad you have been convinced of this. And then he said the third most memorable line I heard. *"Hitler kaputt."* Well, I thought, the next time a son of a bitch like him shows up, maybe you won't be so quick to cheer.

Fontainebleau

I

AIR RAID

It was December 1944. We were a group of replacements traveling across France—no, we were a group of replacements being shipped across France on our way to the front. We were shipped mostly by train, packed in narrow boxcars called 40 and 8s, designed, we were told, for 40 men or 8 horses. These boxcars moved very slowly with frequent delays and stops. But when they stopped and you jumped off to relieve yourself by the side of the tracks, you had to be alert because without warning the train could suddenly take off again and leave you behind.

We were in the boxcars for three days and sleep was a big problem. You had to sleep in a sitting position because if you stretched out on the floor, your legs would lie on top of the legs of the guy sitting against the opposite wall.

We fetched up, as the English say, late one afternoon at a repot depot *(ree-poh dee-poh)* in Fontainebleau. It was a large two-storied, armory-type building. The bunks were double, made of wood, with straw for the bedding, and with a board running alongside the straw so it wouldn't fall out. We carried our own blankets in our duffel bags. A Frenchman told me later that this building had been used by the Germans as a training center for officers. I wondered if I were lying on the same straw a German officer had slept on or had they changed the straw since?

Fontainebleau was great living. We had electricity, lights. We had heat. We had indoor plumbing. And we were to have three hot meals a day instead of cold K rations. Nobody was complaining.

That first night, just before ten o'clock, we were all lounging around on our beds. Lights were still on. Suddenly we heard the droning of a plane's engine in the black sky overhead. I was bunking upstairs. Near the top of the stairs, on the lower bunk, was a sergeant. He was permanent here, a member of the cadre that ran the building.

"Air raid! Air raid!" this cadre sergeant screamed. "Turn off those fuckin' lights!"

The lights were turned off. Somebody turned on a flashlight.

"Turn that fuckin' light off!" the sergeant yelled. The light was turned off before he said off. "I'll shoot the next stupid bastard who turns on a fuckin' light!"

Wow! That was pretty drastic. I guess he had a weapon. No replacement did. We hadn't been issued weapons.

"Put out your cigarettes!" the sergeant bellowed. "They can see those!"

I was on the bottom bunk. The guy on the bunk above me came hurtling down and frantically started putting his shoes and socks on. I was just about to do the same and then I thought, If we're going to be blown up, what good will it do to have your shoes on? My natural laziness took over and I stayed put.

This was our first contact with the enemy and he had the upper hand. We were lying here at his mercy. We listened intently to the droning and waited with pounding hearts for the bombs to drop. It was thrilling and scary.

And then all hell broke loose. There was a tremendous din. We jerked involuntarily when we heard it. Anti-aircraft guns were firing all around our building. They sounded like they were positioned just outside our walls. They filled the sky with exploding shells. We could no longer hear the droning. Then after a seemingly long time, the ack-ack guns took a breather. We could hear the droning again. They hadn't gotten him. It sounded like he was circling around. And then the droning faded away into the distance.

Whew! We could breathe again and murmurs broke the deathly quiet of the floor.

Subsequently we learned that the attacking force in the air raid consisted of a lone unarmed German observation plane. He came punctually every night just before ten o'clock. We called him Bed-Check Charley. When we realized he was no danger to us, we thought of him as a damn nuisance and cursed him because he disrupted whatever we were doing and caused us to turn the lights off. He must have been a damn nuisance for the anti-aircraft boys, too. Every night they fired away and missed.

Why did the cadre sergeant carry on so that first night? I suppose he wanted to have some fun with us.

And yet, even after we knew the plane posed no risk to us, we heard him with a certain unease. Hearing an enemy aircraft over your head states your vulnerability. Was this the night he would drop a bomb?

II
DOLLARS

Our very first morning there, right after breakfast, we were all called together downstairs. The building was run by a cadre of four, the sergeant who slept upstairs, and a corporal and two PFCs who slept downstairs. This meeting was called by the corporal and the two PFCs. The sergeant had disappeared somewhere. The corporal stood on a chair at one end of the building. He was flanked by the two PFCs. We all stood close together in front of him in between two rows of double bunks.

"Fellows," the corporal said, "you probably have brought in some American currency with you from the States. Army regulations require that you trade in your American dollars for French francs. If you are caught with any American money on you, you will face an immediate court-martial. It's a very serious charge because you'll be accused of black-market operations. Guys have been getting sentences of five and ten years for that. So be smart. Protect yourself. Don't be caught with any American dollars.

"The commanding general has authorized this repot depot to be an official currency-exchange center. Line up and turn in your dollars. They'll be exchanged at the official rate of fifty francs to the dollar. This is your first and last chance. After today, it will be your ass."

The two PFCs unfolded a card table and the corporal took his chair and sat behind it. Two shoe boxes suddenly appeared on the table. One was filled with francs. The other was empty. One PFC stood at each side of the table.

The transactions began. Each man in turn announced the amount in dollars he had, laid it down on the table, the corporal counted it out, then reached in his francs box for the correct equivalency, pushed it toward him, then put the soldier's money in the dollar box.

I studied the corporal. Coal-black-haired, glittery-eyed, with the skin pulled tight over his high cheekbones, he had a big-city rat face and a cold, hostile manner to go with it. I didn't trust him. I wouldn't believe him if he swore on ten Bibles.

I looked at the two PFCs. They were watching us like bank guards. And there was an air of suppressed excitement about all three of them, both Rat Face and his two henchmen. They were taking too great an interest in what was going on. Nobody does the Army's work with this kind of intentness. They were personally involved. I didn't know what their game was, but there was something fishy going on. Of that I was certain. I didn't know where that money was going, but I knew where it was not going. It was not going to the Army. I felt we were sheep, being shorn.

American money wasn't any good to us in France. I would be glad to get more francs. But I didn't want to be played for a chump. I slipped unobtrusively out of line and went upstairs. But I was observed. A short time later one of the henchmen appeared at my bed.

"You don't have any American dollars?" he said insinuatingly.

"No," I said. "I lost them all in a card game."

I looked him straight in the eye. Fuck you, Jack. I didn't come all the way over here to be jerked off by you.

He looked at me, unbelieving, and nodded.

They could find out my name and it's never a good idea to fuck around with guys who run things, and I would probably live to regret it, but I was sore.

That night I went out to a café and I was sitting by myself at a table, sipping a cognac, when a soldier approached me.

"Do you mind if I sit down?" he said.

"No," I said. "Go ahead."

There were empty tables in the place so he clearly didn't have to sit here.

"Are you at the repot depot?" he asked.

"Yes."

"You fellows just get in?"

"Yes. Last night."

He nodded.

"I'm a truck driver. I'm with the Quartermasters."

"Oh," I said politely.

"Say, do you have any American money?"

"No, I don't," I said quickly.

I was alarmed. What kind of a question was that to ask a guy out of the clear blue? Was he an undercover agent working for the Army and tipped off about me by Rat Face? Had he followed me from the repot depot? I saw a court-martial ahead.

"If you had any, I'd give you eighty francs on the dollar. The official rate is fifty francs on the dollar."

"Why do you want dollars? What do you do with them?"

"I sell them to the French."

So that was the cadre's game!

"What do they do with them?"

"They put them under their mattress. To the French, dollars are like gold. They have no faith in their own currency. They think the franc is gonna be worthless so they want something that's gonna hold its value. They go crazy for dollars."

Jesus. Those cadre guys really made a killing on us. And without any doubt they did the same thing with every group that passed through.

"Look. I'll be straight with you. I'll give you eighty francs on the dollar but I'm gonna turn around and take that dollar to Paris and I'll get a hundred and ten francs for it. But I can get to Paris and you can't. So I'm taking advantage of the situation. I go to Paris all the time."

"Well, I wish I could help you out, but I don't have any."

"I tell you what. Even if you don't have any dollars, you can still make a little money. Spread the word around to your buddies. Every dollar you bring me, I'll give you a ten-franc bonus on top of the eighty."

"So that's ninety francs on the dollar?"

"Right."

"How will I contact you?"

"I'll come by here tomorrow night."

I nodded. I was thinking. I was thinking this guy was not an undercover agent.

"So that's ninety francs on the dollar?"

"Right."

"How much would sixty dollars be?"

"That's fifty-four hundred francs."

"Okay. Let's see the fifty-four hundred francs."

"Why? You got sixty dollars?"

"Yes."

"On you?"

"On me."

"Great," he said.

He immediately pulled out a roll and peeled off fifty-four hundred francs.

I took out my wallet and gave him my entire supply of green— sixty bucks.

"Ask around," he said. "See what you can come up with."

"I will. How much can you handle?" I was just curious.

"I'll take as many dollars as you can get. I'll buy any cigarettes, too."

I wasn't going to sell him my cigarettes. I didn't have that many. "How much?"

"A hundred francs a pack. That's two bucks a pack."

I didn't tell the fellows about this guy. What good would it do? It would only make them feel bad. And it would look like I was crowing.

The next night the truck driver showed up. I had to tell him I had been unsuccessful. He took it in good spirits and even bought me a drink. We parted on good terms.

III

LE LIT DE MARIE ANTOINETTE

I liked Fontainebleau. I liked wandering around its streets.

Before I entered the service, I hadn't done any traveling to speak of. The Army made it possible for me to see a number of cities for the first time. And it's strange. When you go into a city for the first time and walk around and look at the buildings and the people, that city affects you like meeting a person for the first time. Cities have an aura. In some cities you feel buoyant and hopeful; in others you feel gloomy and depressed. What does this? Is it the way the streets are laid out? Is it the buildings? Is it the presence or absence of greenery? Is it the look on the people's faces, their manner of speaking, their apparent contentedness or their lack of same? Is there something in the air? What makes one city pleasing and interesting and another not? Does it come down to charm? Boston had charm. Chicago had charm. San Francisco, my favorite, had the most charm of all. Oklahoma City had no charm. Detroit made you want to sprint to the bus station for the first bus out of town.

But I liked Fontainebleau. I was comfortable there. I felt at home. The town was somewhat threadbare from the secondary effects of the war but the war itself had bypassed it. There was no war damage, no forlorn piles of bricks.

In one of my first afternoon sorties into town, I saw a group of five or six French people walking down the street. They were talking animatedly to one another. They seemed to be going someplace. On a hunch I followed them at a discreet distance. They led me to a very imposing building. I followed them up the steps. We waited just inside the door. Several American servicemen joined us. They were not from the repot depot.

It turned out we were waiting for a guided tour and we were in a castle where for centuries French royalty had lived.

The guide showed up shortly. He was a small, white-haired, frail old man with erect posture. I wondered if he had been a soldier in the First World War.

We started off. The names rolled off his tongue. This place gave me an overwhelming sense of history. Louis XIV had once sat here surrounded by his courtiers. Louis XVI had once slept here before they dragged him off to the guillotine. Napoleon had once walked on this very same floor where I now stood.

Two things impressed me the most. One was a room with beautiful tapestries on the wall. The second, and most impressive of all, was the *Salle de Bal.* This was a ballroom with a magnificently decorated ceiling but the ceiling did not affect me as much as the breathtaking perfection of the inlaid wooden floor.

We walked on.

"Le boudoir de Marie Antoinette," the guide intoned.

"Le lit de Marie Antoinette."

We stood before her bed. It was protected by a velvet rope on stanchions that kept everybody several feet from the bed. The bedspread was paper thin. One more washing and it would disintegrate.

Suddenly a fat-assed sergeant broke from the group, stepped over the velvet rope, and lay down on Marie Antoinette's bed. He grinned stupidly at everybody. All I could see were his big dirty clodhoppers on that delicate covering. His buddy had a camera and took his picture.

"Monsieur! Monsieur!" the guide remonstrated but he could do little other than be distressed.

When the sergeant got good and ready, he got up and joined the group.

What an asshole. Why was it that so many Americans were assholes?

It was a brief tour. The guide took us to only a few rooms. The castle was an immense, sprawling structure. It would have taken hours to do it justice.

There was no charge for the tour, but the guide stood by the door as we filed out, hoping to be tipped. I gave him a good tip. I noticed that the fat sergeant gave him nothing. That figured.

IV
FINI

I had a favorite café. I went there every night. It was where I had met the truck driver. It was run by a husband and wife. All the work was done by the wife. She was the bartender, waitress, and cashier. He did nothing but play the accordion.

Everyone called her Moo-moo. She was an attractive woman of about forty. She was lively, cheerful, friendly, energetic, indefatigable, and intelligent. She maintained her good humor no matter what, despite all the sexual innuendoes from the soldiers who didn't seem to understand that she was a virtuous married woman.

All the customers were American soldiers. They sat around the tables in the large front room. The front room was where the bar was and this was Moo-moo's territory. I used to go in and get a drink from Moo-moo and then take it to a table in the backroom. This was a smaller, more intimate kind of setting. Here in the backroom her husband sat at a table playing his accordion. I loved his playing. I was starved for music. I wasn't much of a drinker. I could nurse a drink for quite a while. I wasn't here primarily for the drinking. I was here for the music and to get away from all the double bunks. I always ordered cognac, at one hundred francs a glass. I could have had anisette or a peach or apricot brandy.

One night I was in the backroom, relaxing, smoking, sipping my cognac, enjoying the music. There was a husky sergeant two tables away. It was just before closing time. In England in the pubs just before ten o'clock, the bartender would say, "Time, gentlemen. Drink up, please."

Moo-moo stuck her head in the room.

"*Fini! Fini!*" she called out.

"No *fini!*" the sergeant responded.

He drew attention to himself. Moo-moo came over to his table.

"*Fini! Fini!*" she repeated.

"No *fini!* I want another drink!"

"*Fini!*"

"I want a *coe-nee-ack!*"

"*Fini!*"

"I'm not leaving this goddamn place till I get a drink!"

Moo-moo reached over and took his empty glass. With her dish-towel she started wiping off the table.

He stood up. His right fist shot out and he caught her flush on the chin. She went over like she had been poleaxed. He walked slowly out.

Her husband, terribly distraught, rushed over. She was sprawled on the floor. He helped her to her feet. She couldn't speak. She was in a daze.

I felt ashamed of our uniform. Had any German ever slugged her? In her mind, were we worse than the Germans?

V

COFFINS

My friend Berseglaria came up to me and said, "Guess where I was this morning?"

"I don't know. Where?"

"Some Frenchman was nosing around in the woods just outside of town. He was looking for firewood and he saw this place where the ground had sunk a little bit. So he came back to town and got two friends and some shovels and they proceeded to dig it up. It was a pit. They found twenty-six bodies in there, thrown on top of one another. They were French civilians. They had been shot by the Germans. So they took the bodies out and stretched them out on the ground. What a sight!"

"You were there?"

"Yeah, I was there."

"Will you take me out there? I want to see that."

"No, no, no," Berseglaria said, shaking his head. "You don't want to do that, Charley. It's nothing you want to see. It'll make you sick to your stomach. And there's a terrible stink. It was the worst thing I ever saw in my life."

So I didn't go.

That night I talked to Moo-moo about it. My three years of high-school French made it possible for us to have a decent conversation.

"Nobody knows who they are or why they were killed," she said somberly. "Tomorrow afternoon we're going to have a mass funeral for them, from twelve to three. The whole town is going to go. All the businesses will be closed. I won't open till seven o'clock."

The next morning I happened to be walking by the town square when I noticed colorful baskets of flowers on the sidewalk in front of the mayor's office. I went over to have a look and then I noticed beyond the flowers were coffins neatly stacked on the sidewalk.

The coffins were made of plain wooden boards and looked like they had been hastily assembled. Each coffin was a rectangular box, except for the head, which had the corners cut off. Each stack contained three coffins. There were eight such stacks and then I came to something that absolutely staggered me. At the very end of the line were two coffins, one of top of the other, two little coffins. A child was in each of those coffins and a small child at that, maybe no more than six years old.

It's one thing to read about the Germans. It's another thing to have their work in front of your face. And I realized that the French and other captive peoples knew the Germans; Americans had been spared that knowledge. What kind of monsters were the Germans that they would execute small children?

2

Berseglaria

WE WERE AT FONTAINEBLEAU for ten days. Then we were trucked further east to Tent City. It could have just as easily been called Mud City, for Tent City was several lines of tents in a field of deep mud.

Berseglaria and I were on our way to chow. We had to cross the field to get to the kitchen. It was slow going. The mud sucked our feet down and we had to laboriously pull each foot free. They popped out of the mud with a slurping sound.

"Do you know what this mud reminds me of?" Berseglaria asked me.

"No, what?"

"A girl's pussy. Do you know when you've been screwing a girl all night long and you've come three or four times and her pussy is full of your come and hers and then you pull out and it makes a noise just like this—" and he pulled his foot out to demonstrate.

We passed our latrine. It was a fresh-air, six-holer outhouse. It had no ceiling or walls.

A grizzled old Frenchman was sitting on one of the holes.

"The sergeant told us to run off any Frenchies that try to use our latrine but I couldn't do that," Berseglaria said. "How can you go up to a guy in the middle of a shit and say, 'Finish your shit somewhere else'?"

Yesterday morning I had been sitting on an end hole when an old crone came and hiked her skirt up and pulled her underpants down and sat down next to me. I looked at her and she gave me a toothless grin. I wanted to say to her, "Lady, there's six holes here. Why do you have to pick the one next to me?" I couldn't go with her sitting so close so I left. Then I came back later.

"Why do they go to all the trouble of coming over here and using our latrine when they all have an outhouse in their backyards?" I complained.

"Well, they say the French are a thrifty people so this is like a free shit, courtesy of Uncle Sam," Berseglaria said. "And maybe they're hoping for company. If they go at home, they're all alone in their outhouse and that can be pretty lonely. Here they're probably hoping a friend will sit next to them and they can have a nice, enjoyable conversation."

We got to the kitchen, a large tent open on one side for serving, and got a hot meal but had to eat it close by standing up in the mud and being careful not to let the wind upset our food. Then we dipped our mess gear in three garbage cans, the first filled with hot soapy water, the second, a rinse, in less soapy water, and the third, a rinse, in what was supposed to be clear, clean water but wasn't. Then we hustled back to our tent because it was getting dark.

The three hot meals we got every day in Tent City were very important. For those few minutes of each meal, we experienced warmth. The rest of the time we were miserably cold. We were at Tent City for seven days and we never really warmed up the whole time. It was not a freezing cold. It was a raw, damp cold that penetrated to the bone no matter how many clothes we had on. At night when we went to bed, so to speak, we took our shoes off but kept our socks on and lay down wearing our field jackets and overcoats.

The nights were long in Tent City. They started too early, soon after five o'clock. And there was absolutely no place to go. We were next to a small village and at night it became a cemetery. There wasn't a light on in the whole place. We had to retire to our tents and our tents had no electricity or lamps of any kind. Without lights we had to go to bed early. The tents had no beds so we had to lie on the ground inside the two blankets we had brought. The ground was not muddy like it was outside the tent but it was still wet.

We could have lain there in silence in the pitch-black darkness with our eyes wide open, thinking unpleasant thoughts and waiting for the long minutes to pass. Nobody wanted to do that. We could only hope that somebody, anybody, would talk and make the night bearable. Thank God, we had Berseglaria in our tent. He was a blessing in that he loved to talk and he had an inexhaustible supply of stories. With him present, there would not be that dreaded silence. We listened happily to him. He made the time pass and he kept us from thinking our own thoughts.

I had good tent mates. Strange, how things change. When I was in Fontainebleau, I wanted to get away from everybody. But here I was glad they were with me and I wasn't alone.

There were four of us in that tent. Berseglaria and I slept in our half and Browny and Chief slept in the other half. We were all lying close but it was a fairly roomy tent, not like a pup tent. You could stand up in it.

It occurred to me that the four guys in my tent could constitute the nucleus of a squad in a Hollywood war movie. There was me, the bespectacled college boy. There was Berseglaria, the Italian from Brooklyn who loved the Dodgers. We had to fudge that one a little bit. Berseglaria wasn't from Brooklyn and he didn't love the Dodgers, but he was Italian and he was from a big city. There was Browny, the slow-talking, unsophisticated, sweet innocent from the rural South. Browny was perfect for the part. He wouldn't have to act. And there was Chief, a taciturn, full-blooded Indian, the necessary exotic. What we lacked was the poet-philosopher, a character from a Maxwell Anderson–type play, an irritant who could look up at a starry sky and deliver overripe lines with appropriate solemnity, someone who could utter ersatz profundities in a voice-over.

Berseglaria and Browny had come with me from Fort Sill in the States. Chief we picked up along the way. Chief was a slightly built, yellowish-complexioned Hopi. I didn't like calling him Chief so I asked him his name and he willingly told me and I called him that from then on, which he appreciated, but he was known as Chief by all.

As we lay in our blankets, Berseglaria said, "I'm never going out with that Spenser again. That dumb shit. Somebody told him all French women are whores and he believes it. When we were in Fontainebleau, I was walking down the street with him and we came to this house. This lady had her head stuck out the window. She was on the second floor. She was hanging out her wash on a clothesline. If you took a look at the clothes, you'd see she had at least two kids, one a baby in diapers and a little girl.

"Spenser looks up at her and he calls up to her, *'Voulez-vous coucher?'*

"'Shut up, you damn fool!' I says. 'Can't you see she's a respectable married woman?'

"He just laughs."

"What does that mean?" Browny asked.

"How about a fuck?"

"Well, actually it means, 'Would you like to go to bed?'" I said pedantically.

"What's the difference?" Berseglaria said.

"It's just a nicer way to put it," I said.

"I'll tell you one thing," Berseglaria said. "You say that to an Italian wife, you better run for your life. She'll slice your dick off unless her husband slices it off first."

Everybody laughed.

"How long do you think it'll be before our mail catches up to us?" Browny wondered aloud.

"Probably next July," Berseglaria said sarcastically.

No one said anything for a while. All I could see in the darkness was the lit end of Berseglaria's cigarette.

"I was walking around in Southampton one night," Berseglaria said, "and I got lost. I ended up down at the waterfront. It's like a desert island around there. There's not another human being down there. I wanted to get out of there but I didn't know how. I didn't know if I should try to go back or keep going, so I decided to keep going. So I'm walking and it's really dark and creepy. There's this narrow alley between two buildings up ahead. I didn't know it was there till later, but just as I come up to it—I'm in the middle of the sidewalk—this . . . this thing jumps out at me from the alley, lands right in front of me, blocks my way, scares the shit out of me. I thought, I'm going to get robbed! I get ready to fight.

"This thing had matted hair. It had wild, burning eyes. I'll tell you what it reminded me of. I saw a painting once in a book. This guy had just died and was arriving in hell. So these fiends are welcoming him to hell. They surround him and there's fire shooting up behind them and they all have this crazy, maniac face. And this thing in front of me looked just like one of those fiends. I couldn't tell if it was a man or a woman. I couldn't see the shape of its body. It was wearing about three coats and they looked like it had been sleeping in them on the street. They were incredibly wrinkled and dirty.

"The face was bright red, like you'd expect to see in hell. And I figured it was paint, make-up, so this had to be a woman. A man wouldn't wear make-up like that."

"What about a clown?" Browny said.

"This was no clown. This had to be a woman. But what she had done was this. She never washed her face. When the make-up faded, she didn't wash it off. She just applied some more over the old. So her face had layers of make-up. It was like a mask. You couldn't see any skin. And it was a scary mask.

"'A pound for a quickie, Yank!' she says.

"'No, thanks,' I says.

"'Come on, Yank! Show me you're a real man!' she says.

"'I don't have to show you anything!' I says.

"'You're no man!' she says.

"She's sneering at me. What is this? Did I deserve to be insulted by an ugly whore?

"'I'm a man,' I says, 'but are you a woman?'

"'I'll bet you suck wangs!' she says.

"'Not as many as you!' I says.

"'Bugger you, Yank!' she says.

"'Who gets the pound, you or me?' I says.

"And I step around her and start walking away.

"'You can kiss my royal arse!' she yells after me.

"'Pull your pants down and I will!' I yell back.

"'You bloody bahstad!' she yells.

"'When's the last time you took a bath?' I yell.

"I hear all these curses and boy, could she swear. I never heard anybody swear as good as she could and then a rock comes whizzing by my head. I wanted to go back and punch her in the nose, but I knew that if I just touched her, I'd get some kind of rare disease, so I kept going . . . .

"I've been thinking about this and I think I figured out what's going on. It's a plan of the English government. They've got one smart government over there. The government wanted to stamp out V.D. So what they did was go to every fuckin' nuthouse in England and take the women inmates out and have them walk the streets as whores. Nobody in their right mind is going to touch one of these women. So no screwing is going on. No screwing, no V.D."

"What if you're drunk?" Chief said.

"Nobody could be that drunk," Berseglaria said.

"Do you remember when we were in England," Browny said, "and all the kids kept asking us, 'Any goom, choom?' That was funny." He repeated it. "Any goom, choom?" He started to laugh in remembrance.

We crossed the Atlantic on the *Queen Elizabeth* and put in at the Firth of Clyde. Then we came down Scotland on a passenger train. At every stop, swarms of Scottish kids suddenly appeared, beseeching us for gum. We gave what we could but soon ran out. We had fun among ourselves imitating the kids. "Any goom, choom?"

Scotland was a shock. I was expecting the Scotland of Robert Burns and Robert Louis Stevenson, green hills and lovely lakes.

> *O ye'll tak' the high road and I'll tak' the low road,*
> *An' I'll be in Scotland afore ye;*
> *But me and my true love will never meet again*
> *On the bonnie, bonnie banks O' Loch Lomond.*

But there was no Loch Lomond. Instead we went from one industrial city to another, all of them drab and dreary.

"I don't know how the English people can smoke those cigarettes, Players," Chief said. "They taste like horse shit."

Nobody spoke for a while and then Berseglaria started up again.

"When I was in Fontainebleau," he said, "I was walking down the street and I met this G.I. He was going the other way.

"'Do you want to get laid?' he says. 'I know where there's a whore-house.'

"'No, I don't think so,' I says. Then I thought about it. 'Okay, where is it?' I says.

"He gives me the directions and it's right where I was headed anyway so I thought I might just look the place over out of curiosity. I had no intention of going in. You see, I had never been to a whore. I look upon going to a whore as a personal insult. It's like saying, 'This is the only way you can get a piece of ass, by paying for it.' Well, I pay for it, too. But I don't hand her the money. I spend it on her. I show her a good time. I take her someplace. Maybe to a floor show. And sometimes you get nothing for your money. That's just the breaks of the game. But going to a whore, that's like a business transaction. That's like going to the store and buying a pound of hamburger. 'There's the money, now give me the hamburger.' 'There's the money, now spread your legs.' Where's the romance? Where's the suspense, not knowing if you're going to get it or not? Where's the challenge? Where's the fun? Whores never appealed to me. Whores do it for a living. There's no feeling there. But you take a thirty-five-year-old married woman. Her husband's in the service and she hasn't had a fuck since he left. You touch her and she starts to vibrate. You love her up a little bit and she's about ready to collapse. There's no comparison with a whore.

"So I come to this house. It's on a side street. It's the whorehouse. It's got three floors and there's a line of G.I.'s winding around on the backstairs. I ask a guy what's going on and he tells me. The whores are two sisters and they live on the third floor. So there's a lot of us and only two of them, so you have to wait your turn.

"So just for the hell of it, I get in line. I had nothing better to do. It was going to be a while so I had plenty of time to make up my mind. I could leave at any time.

"So I'm standing there in line and I'm thinking about it. I said to myself, 'What the hell am I doing here? I'm going to leave. My heart's not in this.'

"Then I start arguing with myself.

"'Now wait a minute,' I said. 'Don't make any hasty decisions. Think about it. You don't know what the future holds for you. You don't know where you're going or what might happen to you. This could be the last piece of ass you'll ever have. Are you sure you want to pass it up? You don't want to be out there someday regretting that you didn't take advantage of the opportunity. Now it's a whore, so you know it's just going to be a so-so piece of ass. But what's better, a so-so piece of ass or no ass at all? I don't know about you, but if it was me, I'd take the so-so piece of ass.'

"So I lost the argument. I decided to stay.

"Every few minutes a guy comes down the stairs. Every one of them looks away from us, like he's embarrassed and ashamed. I wanted to say to them, 'Why did you do it if you feel that way about it?'

"So we're slowly working our way up. I started halfway between the first and second floors. By now I'm on the landing of the second floor. And I look into this guy's apartment. He doesn't have any curtains or shades whatsoever on the windows so you can look right inside. And this family is sitting in the kitchen. We're right outside their window. But they're paying no attention to us whatsoever. There's a line of soldiers on their stairs every night so I guess they got used to it. But this is one bare kitchen. You expect to see food in the kitchen but there's not one crumb of food anywhere. There's no bowl of fruit on the kitchen table like my mother always had. There's no bread sitting on the breadboard, waiting to be cut. There's absolutely nothing to eat, so I figure, This is a poor family.

"It's a small family. There's the father. He's about thirty. And there's the mother. And there's a little girl, a very serious-looking little girl, maybe six years old. The three of them are sitting at the kitchen table; they're all on the same side of the table. The father is at one end, the mother is at the other end, the little girl is in the middle, and they're just having a quiet conversation. The father says something, and the little girl and the mother look at him. Then the mother says something, and the little girl and the father look at her. Then the little girl says something, and the mother and father look at her. Everybody is listening to the other person, and I thought, This is really nice. This is a family. They're together.

"And then I suddenly realized, This guy has what I want. This guy has a family. That's what I want. I want a wife. I want a little girl or a little boy; I don't care which. I don't want to go through life screwing every dame that chances by. That's no kind of life. This guy has a family. And what have I got? I'm in line with twenty other dogfaces waiting my turn to screw a whore, that's what I've got.

"Well, eventually I get to the head of the line, and the door opens and a guy steps out and the whore is holding the door open for me. I go in. She takes me to this bedroom.

"She's not bad looking, about forty. And I have to give her credit. She's nice. I know she's in a helluva hurry but she doesn't act that way. But she moves right along. She has me take off my clothes. She's wearing a dressing gown. It has blue flowers on it. And she has me sit on the edge of the bed and she brings over a basin of water. But I forgot something. When I stepped in her bedroom, the first thing she wanted was her money—five hundred francs. When I gave it to her, she said, *'Alley oop!'* What's this? She reads the comics? But I don't think so. I think it means 'Let's go!' in French. Am I right, Charley?"

"I don't know. I never heard that expression before."

"So she brings over a basin of water and she starts washing my dick. She has a little tiny piece of soap. But while she's washing my dick, she's examining it very carefully. She's like a doctor, looking for sores. And every now and then she milks it down to see if I have the clap. Then she dries me off with a frayed towel. She takes the basin away and puts a rubber on me.

"*'Alley oop!'* she says.

"She takes her dressing gown off. She's standing in front of me stark naked except for one thing. She's wearing these huge kneepads. What is she going to do, play basketball? I start to laugh and she looks at me funny.

"Her tits were nothing special but she had a nice meaty ass. I've always said that the ass is the last thing to go on a woman. I can show you women of fifty. Their tits have gone but they still have a beautiful ass.

"I couldn't figure out why she was wearing the kneepads and then I find out. She gets on top and her knees are digging into the bed. If she did that fifty times a night, the skin on her knees would have been burnt clean off. Talk about floor burns. And this is one smart girl. If she was on the bottom, think of the pounding she would take, all that banging around. This way she controls it. She saves a lot of wear and tear on herself.

"She's grunting and groaning. She's so hot she can't stand it. Her eyes are rolling around in her head but every now and then she sneaks a glance at me to see how I'm taking it. See, she figures if I think she's excited, I'll come all the faster. She's moaning, 'Euuuuuu . . . . Aaaaaahh.' She's going to pass out. She's fainting with pleasure. It's the screw of a lifetime for her. You'd think I was the world's greatest lover and all I'm doing is laying there, not moving. Then she brings out her big guns. She starts shrieking. This is too much for me. She has got to be the world's worst actress. I start laughing and I can't stop. I start to lose my hard-on. I know when I'm licked. I tell her to get off and I start putting my clothes on.

"'What's the matter?' she says to me in French. I don't know French but I know that's what she said. I could tell she felt bad about it. Maybe she was afraid I'd ask for my money back.

"'Don't worry about it,' I says. 'It's not your fault.'

"That's the first time I've been with a woman and didn't come but I didn't feel frustrated or anything. It was just one of those things.

"But I felt sorry for her, being a whore. Think about putting on a performance like that fifty times a night. God, what a lousy job.

"So I left and I'm going down the stairs and this guy asks me, 'How was it?'

"'Great!' I says."

Berseglaria knew how to tell a story. Some people are just born storytellers. Berseglaria was one of them. He saw his life as a series of stories.

"I think the fire's out," Browny said. "I'll start it up again."

"No, don't," Berseglaria said. "I have an idea for tomorrow morning."

The tents came with one piece of equipment. They had a small, rickety stove in the middle of the tent. The stove had a pipe for the smoke to escape that went straight up and out the top of the tent. The stove bore no resemblance to a roaring furnace. It didn't do much good but it was better than nothing. The trouble was with what we had to burn. We did not have any coal or chunks of wood. We had twigs to start the fire and what amounted to kindling wood to sustain it. The fires didn't last long.

The worst part of the day was when we woke up in the morning. Then we were so cold. We lay huddled in our blankets. Nobody wanted to get up. Nobody wanted to leave the warmth of their blankets. Especially since the rule was that the first guy up had to prepare the stove and start the fire.

Berseglaria now turned on his flashlight and got up out of his blankets. He went over and checked the stove. It was cold and empty. He put twigs on the bottom. Then he filled the remaining space with kindling.

Then he produced a roll of toilet paper. He laid it out from the stove to his blankets, several layers of it. Then he twisted the layers together. Then he got back in his blankets.

"Tomorrow morning I'm going to light it from here," he said. "Nobody will have to get up."

Morning came.

Without getting out from his blankets, Berseglaria struck a match and lit the toilet paper. It was like a long fuse. We all cheered as the flame went down the fuse. Halfway to the stove, the flame fizzled out.

Another good idea that didn't work.

3

The Artillery Replacements

SOMEBODY STARTED A BONFIRE of logs at the edge of the field after evening chow. Where he got the logs, I don't know because I didn't see any lying around, but it was a good blaze. I went over to it. There were other guys there. We stood close together, extending our hands toward the fire, enjoying its warmth. This sure beat lying in the mud in our tent in the cold and dark. Browny stood next to me.

A 2 1/2 ton truck drove up on the road and parked close by. I didn't pay it any attention. I guess the driver wanted to get warm, too. I noticed Browny had drifted off somewhere. Then Browny was back, giving me a discreet tug on my sleeve to get my attention.

"Charley," he said in a low voice, "you wanna see something?" His eyes were big with wonder. "There's a bunch of guys sleeping in the back of that truck."

I went over with him to the truck. The light from the bonfire lit up the back enough to see who was in there.

They were sleeping all right and they weren't snoring. They were sleeping the eternal sleep.

"They're not sleeping, Browny," I said quietly. "They're dead."

Browny's expression showed no surprise, so I think he knew. I think he had just been too horrified to say it, unable to even think it.

They were American soldiers. The bodies were piled haphazardly in a high mound. They were all on their backs, face up. None of them had made it to a hospital. They were in full uniform, overcoats on, lacking only their helmets and cartridge belts and weapons. I got this sudden concern: The guy at the bottom of that pile won't be able to breathe and will suffocate to death.

The bodies were rigid, frozen in grotesque poses, the arms thrust out every which way, extended in front like a store-window man-nequin, thrown back like Jesus on the cross. Some had been surprised in the moment of death, their eyes wide open, their mouths awry. Some were sleeping serenely, like they had just laid down for a nap.

There was dried blood, life's blood, just a splatter here, a thin stream there, a generous bucket of it on this one. I stared at each face in turn, trying to commune with the soul behind the face. The men were so incredibly still.

A burly, unshaven fellow saw us standing there looking in the truck and came over to join us.

"It kind of makes you think, don't it?" he said, without bothering to see what we were looking at.

"Are you the driver?" I asked.

"Yeah," he said.

"Does it bother you to drive them around?"

"Naw. It's just a load to me, like any other load. The way I look at it is this. I'd rather be up front driving than be in the back and have some other guy driving me. Right?"

"Right."

"I could be a lot worse off. I got no complaints. I spend most of my time on the road, nobody around to chew my ass out. And when I go to sleep at night, I know I'm going to wake up in the morning. There's a lot of guys out there—" he jerked his thumb to the east "—can't say that."

"What happens to them?"

"They stick 'em in a mattress cover and bury 'em. That's it. They send their personal stuff home. Of course, they go through it first." He laughed. "I've heard of cases where a married guy is carrying around hot love letters from some dame and they don't want to send them home to his wife."

Except for the coffins in Fontainebleau, this truckload of dead men was the first evidence I had seen of the war's human cost. It was a sobering glimpse. I had seen many bombed-out buildings in England and France but this was different. These were bodies. I told Berseglaria about it later.

Berseglaria was like me. He took it in stride. We, the group I was traveling with, were excited and concerned about going to the front but we weren't terribly worried. This was because we had an ace in the hole. We weren't ordinary replacements. We were a special group. We were highly trained artillerymen. We had trained on a basic piece in the field artillery, the 155mm howitzer. We had spent many months firing at targets at Camp Breckenridge in Kentucky and Fort Sill in Oklahoma.

So we were artillery replacements and we knew our gun. We knew that the 155 howitzer had an effective range of up to nine miles. That was our insurance. Because it meant we would be several miles behind the front lines. The Army wasn't going to risk a valuable gun like the 155 by putting it anywhere near the front line.

We used to joke among ourselves. "The only way an artilleryman is going to get hurt in this war is if the projy man drops a shell on his own foot or the breech man closes the breech on the powder man's hand."

Berseglaria gave us his own version of the joke. "Eleanor Roosevelt was visiting this hospital ward of wounded war heroes and there was one artilleryman in there. Eleanor comes up to each bedside and when she comes to the artilleryman, she says, 'And what happened to you, soldier?' And he says, 'I got the clap, ma'am.'"

We knew that the German Air Force was no longer operative. So barring an attack by our own planes, we would be safe. Of course, in the event of a German breakthrough as took place in the middle of December, then all bets were off.

The next day we left Tent City, not all of us, some of us. We lined up and they called off names. Three 2 1/2 ton trucks were parked in front of us. Berseglaria, Browny, and I got called together. We took our duffel bags and got in the back of one of the trucks. They packed us in there and then we took off. We were in the first truck so we could look out the back and see the other two trucks following us. We drove for a while and when we looked out, the other two trucks were gone. They must have turned off somewhere. Now we were a solo act.

We drove and drove. Then off in the distance we heard the faint sound of a booming gun. We looked at each other. This was the first sound of the war we had heard. We drove some more. The gun boomed again, much closer, much clearer. That didn't sound like a 155. Too deep a reverberation. That sounded like a bigger gun. That baffled me. I didn't know we had bigger guns.

Then, lo and behold! We actually came to a 155 howitzer emplacement. It was at the edge of a field right by the road. Our truck driver stopped and got out of the cab. He went over and talked to the guys.

It was our gun! We stared at the guys, willing them to come over and talk to us. We wanted to ask them questions and tell them we were fellow artillerymen. But nobody came over to the truck. They didn't even look at us.

They weren't firing the gun. They were just hanging around. There was one guy sitting on a wooden box, reading a magazine. He never even looked up. I noticed two things. None of the gun crew were wearing helmets. They all had on wool knit caps. That bore out what we felt, that there was no danger in the artillery. And I noticed right by the gun they had put up a tent. Nobody is going to put up a tent if there is danger. You're going to dig a hole. There were no holes here.

Was this where we would get off? We waited for the driver to come over and let the tailgate down but he was in no hurry to do so. He continued talking to the gun crew. They were laughing together. We waited patiently.

Then he came back but he went right to his cab and started up the engine. Okay, so this wasn't our stop. But the 155s were always in batteries. There had to be other guns around here. We were going to one of the other guns.

Away we went. We drove for a while. Off in the distance we heard explosions. Those were not our guns firing. Those were shells landing. They had to be German shells. As we drove slowly along, the explosions got disquietingly louder and clearer. We were going toward them. We weren't driving parallel to the front. We were going toward the front. Something was amiss here. It hit all of us simultaneously. We looked at each other in consternation. Where was this fucking driver taking us?

Then the driver pulled into a farmyard. There was a house on one side of the yard and a barn on the other.

He came around the back to let the tailgate down.

"Okay, everybody out!" he said. "We're going to spend the night in this barn."

We jumped down and quickly surrounded him.

"Where are we going?"

It was no idle question. We were dead serious.

"You're going where you're supposed to go," he said belligerently.

"Where are you taking us?"

"I'm taking you where you're supposed to go."

"Goddamn it! Where the hell are you taking us?"

"I just do what I'm told, same as you."

But he was beginning to wilt. There were more of us than there were of him.

"We want to know, goddamn it!"

"All right, I'm taking you to the second battalion!"

"The second battalion of what?"

"The second battalion of infantry. What do you think?"

"We're not infantrymen! We're artillery replacements!"

"You'll have to take that up with somebody besides me."

"We never had a day's training in the infantry!"

"I don't know nothin' about that."

"Somebody screwed up here!"

"It happens all the time," he said philosophically.

"There's been a mistake made! Who can we see about this?"

"You can see the chaplain," he said, slyly.

That's when I knew our goose was cooked. When a dumb truck driver can make jokes at your expense, then you know there's no hope.

We were stunned.

We were like the man who goes before the judge when everybody has assured him he will get a suspended sentence and the judge says, "I'm setting the date for your execution."

The driver brought out some C ration cans. We had dinner up in the hayloft of the barn. We opened the cans and sat around, sober-faced diners, eating a cold, clammy, and greasy meal, the perfect end to a perfect day.

We spread our blankets out on the hay. I made a pocket out of mine. I spread one blanket out, folded the second blanket over it, got inside the fold, and folded the first blanket over me. Now I was inside a snug pocket.

I couldn't sleep. I was wide awake.

I was in shock. The unthinkable had come to pass. I was in the infantry. How had this happened? What had I done wrong? All my friends at college had landed on their feet. When the Japanese attacked at Pearl Harbor, we all knew the draft was not far behind. Everybody scrambled for advantage. Ideally, they wanted to escape the draft. But if that was not possible, then they wanted to go in as an officer and/or get assigned a cushy job. One boy on my floor, with no interest in dentistry, was admitted to the dental school. That guaranteed him four years of safety. By the time he was a dentist, maybe the war would be over.

Another joined the Naval R.O.T.C. That meant he would be allowed to stay in school long enough to finish his degree and then would go in the Navy as an officer. Another was angling to get in A.S.T.P., the Army Specialized Training Program. He would be in uniform but he would be a student at some college. Another was trying to get in the Army Language School at Monterey in California to study Japanese. They investigated. They plotted. They planned. They had goals. They chased after professors for letters of recommendation. They worked at it.

And what did I do? Nothing. I didn't lift a finger to help myself. I just drifted passively. Let come what may, was my motto. And what came was the infantry. There is always one dumb shit in every group. That was me. Smart in school, dumb in life.

My freshman English instructor was a pacifist. He raved about a play by Irwin Shaw, *Bury the Dead*. He assigned it for reading and we had to write a paper on it. *Bury the Dead* was an antiwar play, a popular theme in the 1920s and '30s, a reaction to the slaughter of the First World War. But I knew the instructor was wrong. He was behind the times. This wasn't 1931. This was the fall of 1941. There were wild dogs abroad. Hitler had quickly disposed of France and was in the process of chewing up Russia. To face Hitler with pacifism as your policy was suicidal. Hitler would just as soon cut your throat as look at you. He had to be stopped. I just didn't want to be the one to do it, that was all.

I had spent a lot of time reading about the First World War, trying to understand it. Did we enter the war to safeguard Morgan's loans? Did the DuPonts, the Merchants of Death, profiteer from the war? Who cares? Screw Morgan and screw the DuPonts and screw my sense of outrage. All that mattered was that I was here now, lying in a barn, listening for explosives. This was reality.

And the things I had read on my own about the Second World War, Hellman's *Watch on the Rhine*, Steinbeck's *The Moon Is Down*, Sherwood's *There Shall Be No Night*. Empty rhetoric and noble sentiments. Words, words, words, words. Meaningless words. Of what use were words to me now? All the fine speeches in the world couldn't help me now. I was in the soup.

I was in the infantry. I was petrified with apprehension. How could I shoot somebody? Not that I had any reluctance to do so. If someone was trying to kill me, I would shoot him in a millisecond. That was no time to be a Quaker. But how could I shoot him if I couldn't see him? With my poor eyesight, I was at a terrible disadvantage. He would see me before I saw him. He would see me clearly and I would see him fuzzy, if at all. I always did poorly at the rifle range.

How had I ended up here? What unlucky star guided my every move? In the artillery we had felt that the infantry was the bottom of the barrel. It was our belief that the Army placed all the dumb guys, all the guys with low IQ's, in the infantry. The bright guys were placed in branches like the artillery where you needed to have more brains. And now here we were. It wasn't the prestige I was worried about but the danger.

The Army fucked us. They tricked us. They lulled us into this fool's paradise, let us think we were artillery replacements, when all along they knew where we were headed. If we hadn't pressured the truck driver, we still wouldn't know. When was the Army planning to tell us?

I should have known better. You can't trust the Army, no matter what promises they make. This was the second time the Army fucked me. When I was drafted, I had mixed feelings about it. What I really wanted was to stay in school and be a student and let the war pass me by. But a part of me wanted to be drafted. I knew that the war was the big event of our time and I wanted to be a part of it. I didn't want to be left out. So I felt a certain excitement at the prospect of being drafted. But I was also worried. I didn't want to be put in harm's way.

When I received my induction notice and was taken by train along with many other potential draftees to Boston, the whole day there was given over to a thorough physical exam. If you passed that, you were sworn in and given a furlough. Two weeks later we were taken by train again to the same induction center in Boston. This day was taken up by a variety of mental and aptitude tests. At the conclusion of the day, you had a private conference with an officer to look over your prospects in the Army.

My name was called. I went into this little room with plywood walls. The middle-aged officer, a captain no less, sat on one side of a table. I sat across from him, facing him. He had my file in front of him. It had many papers in it.

He studied it without saying anything to me. I waited nervously. Then he spoke.

"With your eyes, you're never going overseas," he said. "I'm classifying you as Limited Service." And so saying, he picked up a big rubber stamp and smacked my folder on the outside. Bam! Big red letters. *Limited Service*.

Hallelujah! I could have jumped across the table and kissed him.

Then he started stamping individual papers from the folder. Bam! *Limited Service*. Bam! *Limited Service*. Bam! *Limited Service*. Bam! *Limited Service*.

Those bams were the sweetest music I had ever heard.

This was perfect. I would be in the service but I would not be in danger. Patriotic but safe, the best of both worlds. It was like being 4-F but in the service. I would wear that uniform proudly and I wouldn't tell anybody. Nobody would ever guess. It would be my little secret.

A year and a half later I found myself walking up the gangplank of the *Queen Elizabeth*. All the way across Europe, from one repot depot to another, I kept praying some doctor would open my file and say, "This man has no business being overseas. Ship his ass back to the States at once!" But it never happened.

Berseglaria was lying in his blankets near me. I wondered if he were sleeping or was he like me, going through hell. This was the worst night of my life. I felt real fear, a panic almost.

Then suddenly I thought of something, something so obvious, so logical, that I was dumbfounded that neither I nor any of the fellows had thought of it. If, as we believed, the artillery was a safe branch of service where nobody ever got hurt, then why would they need artillery replacements? Who would we be replacing? No, the artillery did not need replacements and that had never occurred to us. It was the infantry that needed replacements. It was the infantry where guys were getting killed.

My brain was in turmoil. I was agitated. I was in a desperate situation. What could I do to get out of this? I racked my brains for a way out. I couldn't think of anything.

I was caught like a rat in a trap. I remembered the dogs on the top floor of the Pharmacology building back at college. The professors kept those dogs up there in cages for experimentation. At night when you walked across campus, all you could hear was those dogs barking and howling. The dogs knew what was going to happen to them. They were desperately begging for help, for somebody to rescue them, but nobody rescued them, and nobody was going to rescue me either.

The Army had brought me here, slowly, step by step. Maybe it was my destiny to be here and I could not escape it.

This goddamn Europe. A thousand years of unending quarrels behind them, and they were still fighting. This place was a cesspool, beyond redemption. Why didn't the U.S. turn its back on them? Let them kill each other. Why should America sacrifice its young men in fruitless carnage?

I tossed and turned some more. Toward daybreak I fell asleep. Good thing nobody woke us early so I did get a bit of sleep.

We got up and each of us picked out a cold C ration can for a combination breakfast-lunch.

The truck driver said, "I'll be back in a while," and took off in his truck.

We were left to sit around in the barn. Nobody felt much like talking. Even Berseglaria, as talkative as he was, was silent.

"How far away do you think the front is?" I asked Berseglaria.

He frowned and shook his head, meaning he didn't know and didn't want to think about it.

I noticed that the explosions had become more and more infrequent during the night and finally stopped altogether. Today there were no sounds of warfare. Everything was quiet.

In the early afternoon the truck rolled back in. The driver told us to load up. We hoisted our duffel bags onto the truck and climbed in. Off we went. But he drove slowly.

After a while we came to a town. Some of the houses had suffered war damage. We saw a few forlorn-looking G.I.'s here and there. They didn't even look at us.

We came to a large house with a good-sized courtyard. The driver rolled to a stop by the entrance and we unloaded. We went in the courtyard.

There was a whole bunch of guys standing in that courtyard. They had duffel bags at their feet and worried looks on their faces. They were like us, replacements. I didn't recognize any of them. So I knew they hadn't come from Tent City.

We joined the group. Actually it wasn't one solid group. The men had split up into clusters of twos, threes, and fours, guys standing close to their friends. Berseglaria, Browny, and I stood together.

We stood for a long time, waiting. Then a sergeant walked into the courtyard. I couldn't take my eyes off him. He was the dirtiest soldier I had ever seen in my life. He was caked with dried mud from head to foot, dried mud caked on top of dried mud. He had several days' growth of whiskers. His eyes were sunken and had dark circles around them. He walked heavily. He looked exhausted. My first thought was: Wherever this guy's been, I don't want to go there.

I noticed he was wearing shoes and leggings. Leggings were a pain in the ass. All the replacements were wearing combat boots. This was one of the oddities of American supply. The guys in the States, who didn't need them, had combat boots. The guys in combat, who needed them, did not have combat boots.

What gave me pause was his helmet. It had a large dent in it, right in the front. What could have done that? I remembered the sergeant in basic training holding up a helmet in front of the whole platoon and saying, "This here helmet here is made of the finest steel in the world. Nothing can get through it." That dent meant something had not got through it but had come close. It was worrisome. (A short time after this I was to see a pile of helmets gathered for salvage. Some of them had gaping, jagged holes in them.)

The dirty sergeant stood on the other side of the courtyard, away from us. He made no move to come over to us. He just stood there, eyeing us speculatively. I had a feeling he was waiting for somebody or something.

Then another sergeant walked in. This one was different. He didn't look exhausted. He was shaven. And his clothes were nowhere near as dirty as the first sergeant's.

This sergeant went over to the dirty sergeant and they stood there talking, but looking us over at the same time. It reminded me of a cattle auction with the ranchers standing around looking at the cattle.

The clean sergeant was zeroing in on Berseglaria, Browny, and me. I was sure of it because his eyes stayed on us. Then, lo and behold, he left the dirty sergeant and walked toward us.

He came right up to us.

"Any of you guys ever have any radio experience?" he said.

I thought fast. Would it be better to have radio experience or would it be better not to have radio experience? What was I getting into here? Were they planning on dropping me behind enemy lines with a radio? It was like buying a pig in a poke. But I figured next in line was the dirty sergeant. It was better to take my chances with the clean sergeant. I took the plunge.

"I was a radio operator in the field artillery," I said. "That's voice, not code."

He nodded.

"What did you do?"

"Well, sometimes I was at the guns but usually I went with the forward observer in his jeep. He was a first lieutenant. We'd drive out into the country and then he'd stop and take out his binoculars and spot a nice clump of bushes. That would be the target. And he'd try to bracket it. We'd fire one round at a time and he'd watch where it landed and call out corrections and I'd relay them back to the guns. And then when we had closed it up, he'd say, 'Fire for effect!' and we'd wipe out that clump of bushes. And then we'd drive off and look for another clump of bushes. We were a good team. No bush was safe with us."

He smiled.

"You come on with me," he said.

I hoisted my duffel bag up on my shoulder. I looked at Berseglaria and Browny. They had a stricken look on their faces, like I was deserting them, and I was.

"I'll see you guys later," I said.

I hustled after the sergeant. He was already walking away. I caught up to him and walked a half step behind. We went out of the courtyard and down the street.

(His name was Sergeant Drummond and I have no doubt that his plucking me out of that courtyard saved my life. My premonition about the dirty sergeant was right. Everyone of those poor stiffs I left standing there in that courtyard ended up in a rifle company. In a week's time some of them would be dead. *maybe*

(Sergeant Drummond made me a radio operator at the battalion level. The battalion CP [Command Post] was positioned a short distance behind the rifle companies, out of range of small-arms fire. It was a short distance behind, but it was the distance between life and death.)

I followed the sergeant to a house. We went in. There was nobody in there.

"This is where we're going to stay," he said. "If I were you, I'd lay my blankets out on the floor now. That way you'll claim your spot.

"Chow is going to be served in about half an hour. The kitchen is about five houses down the street. Take your mess gear down there."

He left then.

I was sitting on my blankets eating a hot meal when my new mates began straggling in. They nodded at me. They talked hardly at all. They looked dead tired. As soon as they had eaten, they laid out their blankets and went to sleep.

When Sergeant Drummond walked me to this house, I noticed that the house next door to us was burning. Nobody paid it any attention. Nobody was trying to put the fire out.

Our room had an unshaded window facing the burning house. It let in the light of the fire. I lay in my blankets and looked at the opposite wall at the changing pattern of light and shadows as the flames flickered and danced in soundless reflection. In three or four minutes I fell into a deep and peaceful sleep.

4

The First Week

THE NEXT MORNING the fellows were quite different. They were cheerful and joked around. It was due to a combination of things—a good night's sleep, plus a hot breakfast, and, most important of all, they were being given a rest. I saw that I had come at a good time, at the end of something, not the beginning. They were friendly to me, which I really appreciated.

There followed some relaxing days. The house we were in was snug and well built and it had a very effective stove in the living room, which was where we stayed. There was an ample supply of briquets down cellar. These briquets were half the thickness of a brick, light in weight, and had rounded corners. We went down cellar and filled a small wooden box with them and stuffed them into the stove. Our living quarters were cozy and warm.

The only annoyance we had was the presence of the dour owner of the house. He was living elsewhere but he kept lurking around, keeping a suspicious eye on his property. He slipped into the cellar and inspected what he took to be his dwindling supply of briquets. He came upstairs and complained bitterly that we were being wasteful. As far as I could see, we hadn't even made a dent in the mound of briquets in the bin.

The next day he showed up again, angry at our use of his out-house in the backyard. He complained that we were filling up the hole. He then nailed the outhouse door shut. Hillbilly and I were chosen to dig a slit trench in the backyard. Hillbilly was a wire man or a telephone lineman.

As we dug, Hillbilly stopped and said, "I'll be glad when we get back in Germany." We were in Luxembourg. "None of this Allies bullshit. We just tell the Krauts to get the hell out and that's the end of it. None of this fuckin' asking permission.

"And I'll tell you something else, too. The guys in Easy Company are sleeping in a barn. If we were in Germany, they'd be sleeping in a house like us. There wasn't enough houses for them because we couldn't kick the people out. That's for the birds. We're here trying to help these people. They should be the ones sleeping in the barn."

That evening I had occasion to curse the landlord myself. I had to use the slit trench. Now let it be said that an outhouse is a major advancement in civilized living. You sit down in a comfortable, pri-vate setting, sheltered from the elements, and you can relax, take your time, possibly even meditate a little. But when you use a slit trench, you have to straddle it, and you have to be careful in the dark that your foot doesn't slip into the trench, and you crouch down like an animal, without privacy or any dignity or any sense of relaxation, and with an icy wind whipping at your bare ass. I cursed that man.

The following night I had a sudden and terrible attack of the runs. In the middle of the night I woke up with an irresistible urge to defe-cate. I didn't have time to lace my boots. I slipped into them and ran for the slit trench. But I didn't make it. I barely made it to the door. Just outside the house, I dropped my unbuttoned pants that I had been holding up with my hand, squatted, and with great velocity out shot a liquid soup. I groaned. And then I realized I had one more problem. I hadn't had time to put on my helmet, and behind the webbing of the helmet was my supply of toilet-paper squares. I went back and got my helmet, returned to the mess and wiped myself. Then I went in to sleep.

The next morning Sergeant Drummond, who had been sleeping elsewhere, came over early and almost stepped in the puddle. It pissed him off.

He came in and said angrily, "Who the hell took a crap just outside the door? That's disgusting!"

I was still on the floor in my blankets. I raised my head.

"It was me, Sergeant," I said. "I had the runs last night and I couldn't make it to the trench. I'll clean it up."

That seemed to mollify him.

I was embarrassed and hoped I hadn't made a poor impression on him but I couldn't do anything about it now.

Later that day Sergeant Drummond said to me, "There's no room in the radio trailer for your duffel bag so I'm going to take it to Regimental Supply. They'll hold it there for you."

(And so he did. I never saw that duffel bag again. I had lugged it across the ocean, down Scotland, down England, across France, and when I reached my destination, they took it away from me. My duffel bag was crammed with clothing, including two extra woolen O.D. (Olive Drab) shirts and one O.D. pants. I was left with the shirt on my back and the pants I had on. I wore them for the next two months without a break, day and night. At night they served as my pajamas. After the first month the inside of my collar was dyed a greasy black, a mixture of sweat, dirt, and skin oil. So much grime had worked itself into the fabric of my pants that the legs could stand up by themselves. After the two months they took us back to a mobile tent for a hot shower, a spraying of DDT powder on our bodies to discourage lice, and a clean change of clothing.)

I was struck by how congenial the fellows were. Nobody was nasty. There were no arguments. There was no drinking. Of course, there was nothing to drink. And what I really liked was there was no card playing. Card players, grumpy and absorbed, are often a pain in the ass. And if money is involved, then you get the sore losers. Every barracks I ever lived in always had a tense card game at the end of every month, on payday. They played after dinner through the evening and half the night, usually in the sergeant's room where there was no lights-out rule. After three days all the money was in one pocket, but the broke card players continued to play in the evenings, without the tension, for want of anything better to do.

I talked to the fellows a lot. I wanted to know what was going on. I wanted to know what they did, what their duties were. I didn't know anything about the infantry. I wanted to know the structure, the organization, of the infantry.

I learned there were three regiments in an infantry division. Each regiment had three battalions. Each battalion had three rifle companies. In our case, it was Easy, Fox, and George Companies. The rifle companies were the heart and soul of the battalion, the reason for its existence. We were support troops for the rifle companies. I was a member of the communications crew. We were responsible for wire and radio communications to the rifle companies. The wire men laid telephone lines down from the battalion CP to the CPs of the three rifle companies. All the lines went through the battalion switchboard.

I was a radio operator. Each rifle company had its own radio operator. I was a battalion radio operator. The principal radio traffic was between the radio operator at battalion CP and the rifle company radio operators wherever they happened to be.

Battalion aid men were another support group for the rifle companies. The rifle or line companies had their own aid men or medics. These medics gave emergency aid to the wounded on the spot but they had to stay with the company. To get the wounded from the battlefield to the battalion aid station was the responsibility of the battalion aid men. There was one doctor for the whole battalion. He would be at the battalion aid station and give the wounded further emergency care when they were carried in. Then an ambulance would come and take the wounded to the rear to a field hospital.

The doctor was Captain Sawyer. The fellows referred to him, but not to his face, as Doc. Later I found out that he was called Li'l Abner by the officers, again, not to his face. They called him that because he had a shock of black hair and his early years had been spent in a bucolic setting.

We were resting and the rifle companies were resting, too, but the rifle companies were not resting quite like we were. They were taking turns, each company going out for a twenty-four-hour stretch to man a defensive perimeter around the town. At night after we had emptied the box of briquets into the glowing stove and lay down to sleep, cozy in our blankets, warm and dry, a company was outside in the cold and dark, the men half frozen, awake through an endless night, on ground wet with freshly fallen snow.

I learned that there was no one between the battalion and the German troops, who were out there somewhere, just beyond this town. It was like the two sides were taking a time out. They initiated no hostile action against us and we initiated no hostile action against them.

Jelich, a radio jeep driver, said, "I like this. This is the way wars should be fought. We don't bother them and they don't bother us. Everybody minds their own business."

Sergeant Drummond spent a little time with me going over radio procedures.

"When you're giving numbers out, never say 'oh.' Always say 'zero.'"

I knew that.

"Never call Colonel Rudd Colonel Rudd." Colonel Rudd was the battalion commander. "We use code. Always call him Kingfish Major. The exec officer is Kingfish Minor. The CO (Commanding Officer) of Easy Company is Easy One. The CO of Fox Company is Fox One. The CO of George Company is George One.

"Ammunition is called 'apples.' You're going to get a call from one of the line companies for stretchers. Except that we don't call them stretchers. We call them 'bathtubs.' Never say stretchers on the air. We don't want the Krauts to know how many wounded we have."

"Are they listening in?"

"They might be. You never know."

Hillbilly burst into the house one afternoon, all excited.

"We're going to be relieved!" he shouted. "We're going into Regimental Reserve! We're going to pull out!"

A transformation immediately took place. We were giddy with joy. Elation is a heady wine; everybody was grinning and acting silly.

Then somebody thought to ask Hillbilly, "How do you know?"

"I got it from Sergeant Drummond and he got it straight from Lieutenant Tidwell. Tidwell is Intelligence. If anyone is going to know, it's going to be him."

All we had to do was wait for Sergeant Drummond to come over and tell us to load up. We watched for him. He didn't come. Where was he? Why wasn't he coming? What was keeping him? And with every passing hour, the elation oozed out of us.

It had been a most pleasant and relaxing seven days for me. I had no duties. I spent the time talking to the fellows, reading *Stars and Stripes,* the daily Army newspaper, writing letters home, ambling around town for the exercise. I had three hot meals every day and slept every night snug and warm. "This isn't so bad," I said to myself. "So far, so good."

On the seventh day, we had just finished evening chow and were sitting around when Sergeant Drummond suddenly appeared.

"If I were you guys," he said, "I'd turn in now and try to get some sleep. We're going to have breakfast at midnight."

That was all he said and he left.

What a strange time to have breakfast, at midnight. What did this mean? Were we going to be relieved? And they wanted to make the switch during the early-morning hours so that it would not be observed? But I had a sinking feeling that told me that wasn't it.

Suddenly everybody was very quiet. We all lay down on the floor, in our blankets. But I knew I wasn't going to sleep. It was too early. All I could do was change position every so often and wait for the hours to pass. Whatever was going on, wasn't good. I felt sure of that.

About ten minutes to midnight, Sergeant Drummond reappeared.

"Everybody up!" he yelled. "Let's go!"

Everybody got up. Nobody was talking.

We walked down to the kitchen and shuffled in line and brought our breakfast back. It was scrambled powdered eggs, hash-brown potatoes, and oatmeal. I had a canteen cup of hot coffee. I found it undrinkable. It was partly dregs.

5

Crossing the Sauer

AFTER WE HAD EATEN, Sergeant Drummond took me out to the radio trailer. He handed me a radio. I noticed right away that one of the two shoulder straps on it was dangling, broken and useless. I pointed that out to him, but he said, "You'll have to use this one for now."

I put it up on my back as best I could.

"Report to Lieutenant Tidwell," he said to me. "You'll be going with him."

"Where is he?"

"He should be at battalion CP."

I didn't know what Lieutenant Tidwell looked like. I had listened to the fellows talking about the officers, but I hadn't met any of them. They stayed clear of us, which was all right with me.

"Should I go now?"

"Yes."

I knew the house where battalion CP was. I had walked by it during daylight. They had a little wooden sign out front.

I went down there now and hesitantly opened the door. It wasn't a big room and it was crowded with officers. I slipped in and stood at the back. I guessed rightly that these were the officers from the line companies. They were listening intently to Colonel Rudd, who was pointing out places on a large green contour map. The map had a transparency over it and some kind of stiff backing. It was held up by a junior officer who stood behind it and alongside the colonel.

I noticed the colonel had a silver oak-leaf cluster on his collar. He was a lieutenant colonel.

There was an air of great seriousness in the room. There were no jokes, no smiles, no idle conversation. I could feel the tension.

Finally Colonel Rudd finished and there were two or three questions and then the line officers began leaving. Who was left was Colonel Rudd and the battalion staff, six or seven officers. I was wondering who I should ask to point out Lieutenant Tidwell. He saved me the trouble. He came up to me and said, "Are you the new radio operator?"

"Yes, sir," I said.

"All right. You come with me."

I followed him out. There was a long column of infantrymen walking single file down the street. We cut into the line. He was several men ahead of me.

Lieutenant Tidwell was a small man, maybe a couple of inches taller than me. I was five feet four. He had a dapper little black mustache. As I got to know him, I found out that he was energetic, always bustling about, always just arriving or leaving. I got the impression from him that he had had a hardscrabble early life in the backcountry of Kentucky and was surprised and delighted to find himself an officer. He did not see rank as his rightful place in the scheme of things, as some did. My father would say of someone he liked, "He does not put on airs." Lieutenant Tidwell did not put on airs. But, of course, at this point I knew nothing about him.

The line of infantrymen seemed endless, ahead of us and behind us. It wasn't snowing now, but a lot of snow had fallen. It crunched under our feet. It was a clear night. The moon was out. It was cold; the temperature was 16° above zero.

We walked down the street, till the houses ended. Then we were out in the country, beyond the town. We kept walking.

There wasn't one word of talk. There was a deathly silence hanging over these men. Their faces were masks. I had the feeling their eyes were not seeing; they were turned inward.

What was going on? Where were we going? What was I supposed
to do? I had no idea. Nobody told me anything.

There was a certain quality about these men. Something had
been set in motion, some destination, irrevocable. Despite my inex-
perience, I knew what it was. These men were marching to their
death. And they knew it. I felt this in my bones. And then I realized
with ominous dread that I was marching with them.

We came to some woods. They were on our left. After a little
while, we made a sharp turn off the road and into the woods. There
was a trail, maybe eight feet wide. We went down it, and *down* is the
right word, because it sloped like a hill.

I slipped on a patch of ice. My legs shot out from under me and
I went down hard on my ass. Someone took a firm hold of my arm
and helped me to my feet. "Thanks," I murmured. He gave me the
sweetest smile. It pierced my heart.

The line of soldiers continued down the trail. Lieutenant Tidwell
was waiting for me, standing at the side of the trail, on my left. "Over
here," he said. I left the line. I followed him into the woods. He had
found a small clearing. We were close to the trail. We could see who
was on it.

Then he sat down in the snow. I followed suit.

"This is where we're going to be," he said. "The battalion is going
to cross the river and make a big push. They're going to get so far
from the CP that they'll be out of radio range. That's why we're here.
We're going to be a relay station. We'll take messages from the CP
and transmit them to the line companies and vice versa."

"How do they get across the river?" I asked.

"Assault boats."

(The trail was maybe eighty yards long. Lieutenant Tidwell and I
were halfway down it, forty yards from the river and forty yards from
the top.

(As it turned out, I was in those woods the whole day and I never
relayed a single message. The planners had erred on the side of over-
optimism. The battalion never got far enough away from the CP to
require my services. All transmissions came through loud and clear.

(German resistance was fierce, fanatical. Across the river was flat, open ground and then high ground where the Germans had had a long time to prepare defensive positions.)

I was sitting on the snow beside Lieutenant Tidwell with the radio receiver pressed against my ear. The night slowly passed while we waited for the attack to begin. Everything was quiet. No one came down the trail. The infantrymen had all gone down to the river and were hidden just inside the woods, waiting. The assault boats were already there, previously brought down by the engineers.

This infantry radio was quite different from my artillery radio. The artillery radio was big, heavy, with great range. You did not carry it around. It did not have a handset. You spoke into a microphone and the sound came out of a speaker in the radio itself. With the infantry radio the sound came out of the earpiece of the handset. The only way to know if someone was trying to reach you was to keep that receiver to your ear.

Just before daybreak there was a sudden eruption of small-arms fire coming from the direction of the river. The attack had begun. It sounded like two hundred men with rifles and automatic weapons were simultaneously emptying their clips. We have tremendous firepower, I thought.

But we were also being fired upon. Calls came almost immediately for bathtubs or stretchers. Lieutenant Tidwell and I lay flat in case a stray bullet found its way up where we were.

It was unbelievable. Forty yards from me men were dying. My rational mind told me this was happening but emotionally I couldn't believe it. It was just too horrible, too insane. The soldier with the gentle smile who had helped me up—was he at this very moment alive or dead? I fervently hoped he was alive.

The firing continued, then leveled off, then became sporadic.

Maybe thirty minutes after the first shots, Colonel Rudd called Easy Company.

"Lieutenant, are you across yet?"

"No."

"What's holding you up?"

"We had to turn back. We were under heavy fire."

"Where are you now?"

"We're in the woods."

"Lieutenant, you've got to get those men moving. You're holding up the advance."

"These men have had it, sir! They won't budge for me or anybody else! I've tried everything! They won't move!"

I never heard a voice so stressed as that lieutenant's, so anguished, so desperate, so shaken, so tortured.

"Lieutenant, I know it's tough up there, but you're going to have to go over right now. The longer you wait, the worse it'll be. Get all the available boats and go over right now. Quit screwing around."

"We need more time."

"You're going to expose Fox Company's flank. I told you what I want. Now do it. Or I'll get somebody up there who can."

Thirty minutes later the lieutenant called back.

"We're across, sir."

"Good."

That was the whole conversation.

The lieutenant sounded better.

I thought my role in this engagement was to be that of a compassionate spectator. I was quite content to listen in on these fascinating bits of conversation and let it go at that. I did not expect to be dragged into this thing. I was mistaken.

Suddenly there was a whistling in the air and it was coming closer. Lieutenant Tidwell and I had been sitting. We instinctively threw ourselves face down in the snow. It was a German shell, an 88, my very first 88. It passed us by, but not by much, exploding on the other side of the trail. Lieutenant Tidwell and I looked at each other. It was not the look that passes between an officer and an enlisted man. It was the look that passes between two humans who have just narrowly escaped death.

Somebody was trying to kill me. I was in shock. I was the center of the universe. Life could not exist without me. Were these axiomatic truths to be disregarded? Was my death possible? Facing up to your own extinction takes some doing. If they were trying to kill someone else, that I could comprehend. I could even tolerate it. But not when it was me.

The German shelling of these woods followed a pattern: four or five shells one after the other, and then maybe ten minutes of nothing, and then another four or five shells. That was how the morning went.

When an 88 came, I quickly figured out I didn't want to have my arms exposed, so I would hide them under my body. My right arm I bent and put under my chest. My left arm I used as a pillow, pressing my forehead down into it with some vigor.

An 88 overhead produces a moment or two of heart-stopping terror in the likely recipient because it gives a warning. Its whistle ensures that you will have a chance to think about what is about to happen. And there is nothing you can do about it. You are totally helpless. It will land where it wants to land. And another basic-training truth bit the dust. The sergeant stood in front of us and said, "A well-trained soldier will survive. A poorly trained one won't." As far as I could tell, the 88s did not distinguish between the well-trained and the poorly trained soldiers. It killed both impartially.

As we lay there, Lieutenant Tidwell and I heard the most comforting sound in the world, that of our own artillery firing at the German line. Our shells passed high overhead, not whistling, but breaking the air with a decisive rush. "Good!" I said to myself as I heard them. "More! More! Give it to them!"

Lieutenant Tidwell and I were close to the trail. We could see whoever went up or down it. It was mostly stretcher bearers. Calls had come in from the line companies for bathtubs soon after the attack started. There were two teams of stretcher bearers. Each team had four men. There were only a couple of guys available from battalion aid so jeep and truck drivers had been pressed into service as bearers. The team walked down the trail to the river with an empty stretcher. They put a wounded man on the stretcher and carried him back up the trail. It took all four men, one man at each corner of the stretcher. And it was slow going. The snow on the trail had been packed down by all the feet. This hard snow had turned to ice in many spots. Plus they were carrying the guy uphill. It was exhausting work.

At the top of the trail on the road, hidden behind some trees, a jeep and a driver were waiting. The jeep was rigged to carry a stretcher. The bearers set their stretcher in place on the hood of the jeep, lashed it securely, picked up an empty stretcher, and trudged back down the trail to get the next guy. The jeep driver drove the wounded guy to battalion aid where Captain Sawyer gave him emergency care. An ambulance then drove a load of the wounded to a field hospital.

Since Lieutenant Tidwell and I were about halfway up the trail, the stretcher bearers often stopped by us to take a breather. They carefully set the stretcher down and then just stood there for a couple of minutes, breathing hard, resting. Then they picked the stretcher up and continued up the trail.

Sometimes shells came. Once the bearers were right by us. They hurriedly put the stretcher down and dove for the ground. The wounded man lay totally exposed, his face and belly up. I thought: Wouldn't it be ironic if he were hit now? If he could only make it safely to that jeep, he would be out of this thing. Fifty more yards and he would have fifty more years of life. One yard for every year of life.

But I knew that not everybody who made it safely to that jeep was going to make it. Some of the wounded looked in bad shape.

I started thinking about a war movie I had seen when I was a little kid. The wounded soldier is in a hospital bed. He has a splendid bandage around his head. When he comes to, his first words to the nurse are, "What am I doing here? I've got to get back. The fellows need me," and he climbs out of bed, takes three steps, and faints. The doctor and an orderly put him back in bed, while the nurse says, "Poor boy. It's the loss of blood. They're all the same. They all want to get back." The war movies are so full of bullshit. Why do we go to them? Because the bullshit is what we want to hear. We stand in line to hear it.

Three soldiers came up the trail. The one in the middle was bareheaded and weaponless. He had left his helmet and rifle behind. He had been wounded in his right leg, halfway between the knee and hip. Judging from the extent of the bandaging, he had some kind of large-sized wound. Bright red blood was running down his leg. They had cut away the clothing on the leg so that the flesh was exposed.

He could not put any weight on that leg. He was hopping on his left leg, half-supported and half-carried by his two buddies. He had his arms around their necks and they had their arms around his back. They had helmets on and carried their rifles slung.

I looked at the wounded guy with pure envy. The lucky bastard. The wound didn't look to be terribly serious. He was out of it now, soon to be in a hospital bed, safe and looked after. Maybe even to be shipped home, back to the States. I would settle for a wound like that this very instant, I thought, and I'd be thankful.

The two buddies carried him up the trail and all the way back into town and dropped him off at battalion aid. Since they were in town, the two buddies decided they might as well stop off at the kitchen to get some hot coffee and maybe a bite to eat. That's where they were, sitting down, leisurely sipping their hot coffee, when, bad timing for them, Colonel Rudd took a break from the CP and came in to get some hot coffee himself. He exploded when he saw them and blistered their ears and sent them immediately back to their unit.

Colonel Rudd radioed the three line company commanders.

"Absolutely no one in a line company is to assist in the carrying of wounded to battalion aid. Is that clear? The wounded are to get back on their own power or they are to be carried back by the litter bearers. We need every man we have on that line! We can't spare anybody! Pass that order to every man in your command!"

Then Colonel Rudd called me. He wanted to talk to Lieutenant Tidwell.

The stretcher bearers had set a wounded man down on the trail and were standing by the stretcher, resting. Lieutenant Tidwell had gone over to talk to them.

"He's talking to the stretcher bearers, sir. I'll call him over."

"No. Don't bother. Just tell him to get back here. I want him to patrol the road leading into town. I want him to look for infantrymen, with or without any wounded. Turn them back on the spot! Also, check battalion aid and the kitchen for any malingerers."

I relayed Colonel Rudd's instructions to Lieutenant Tidwell.

He was delighted to hear them. I won't say that he ran out of those woods. That would be unkind. Let's put it this way. He left in unseemly haste without taking time to bid me adieu. And who's to blame him? If you were told you could leave an area where 88s were intermittently falling and go to an area where 88s were not falling, wouldn't you move with alacrity, too?

I found out later how Lieutenant Tidwell patrolled the road. He patrolled it sitting on his ass in the warm kitchen, drinking hot coffee, eating snacks, and chatting with everyone who wandered in. Occasionally he strolled over to battalion aid to check and on his way back would look down the road. But he was astute. What better place to lie in wait for malingerers than the kitchen? Where else would a malingerer go?

Shortly after Lieutenant Tidwell left, still in the morning, there was an abrupt change in the German pattern of sporadic shelling. Suddenly the sky was alive with 88s. They came one after the other, without pause. They exploded short of me, beyond me, to my left, to my right, all around me, everywhere but on me. They didn't stop coming. The Germans intended to obliterate these woods.

"I'm going to die here," I said to myself. How could the shells keep on missing me? It wasn't possible. There was no way I was going to leave these woods alive. I was done for. This was my last day on earth. I could see the headstone.

Charles Reis Felix

April 29, 1923–Jan. 18, 1945

And I felt a sudden rage. It wasn't fair! I was too young! I was a student, for God's sake! I hadn't even started to live yet! I had never known love. Since I entered the service, I had made love to a number of girls and women, but the love involved was momentary and counterfeit. I had been in love from afar with girls in school but these were one-sided love affairs that existed only in my mind. I had never had a girlfriend. That was what rankled the most, not to have known love. I was being cheated out of what I already knew to be the most precious experience life has to offer. And now I was never to have it.

All my life my mother and father had told me how lucky I was to have been born in America and not in Portugal. I had a cousin my same age in Portugal. His family was poor. All my life I had heard how much better my prospects were than his, everything better, better education, better food, better medical care, better jobs, better opportunities, a better life. All my life I had heard that and I believed them and now I could see the joke was on me. A better life but a short one and an ending inside a mattress cover. What good was it to live in the land of opportunity if they killed you at twenty-one? Twenty years from now my cousin would be alive, breathing, talking, thinking, walking, eating, sleeping, waking up, looking at the sky, looking at a tree, feeling the warmth of the sun, making love to his wife, playing with his children, and I would be a rotting bag of bones in a depressing military cemetery somewhere in Europe. Who was the lucky one?

America offered you much but it exacted too high a price—your life. My parents had made a terrible mistake coming to America. I would have been better off being born in Portugal. It was better to live in a poor, backward country that was too unimportant to be noticed than it was to live in a rich, powerful country like the United States that couldn't help being drawn into every war that came along.

I was going to an unknown, unremembered grave, just another corpse. Only my family would mourn me, my mother most of all. I saw her face. When I was a child in bed with a fever, she would take a handkerchief and wet it with cold water and lay it across my forehead. She used to make the bed with me in it when I was sick—how I loved that. I would roll over from one side of the bed to the other. And in the first grade when there was an epidemic of nits at school, she examined my head every afternoon when I got home from school. My best friend Albert Costa, his mother cut all his hair off as a precaution. We called that getting a pineapple. But I would sit on the floor by my mother's chair and put my head in her lap and close my eyes and enjoy it, hoping it would never end. She would play with my hair and rub my scalp. It felt so good. I liked it so much that long after the epidemic was over, I used to say to her, "Ma, my hair feels itchy. I think I got some bugs." And I would lay my head in her lap and she would go through my hair, looking for nits. She never found any.

I would never see her again.

The shells continued to come.

It was unbelievable. Two years ago I was at college, lying on the grass in front of the library, watching all the girls go by. I was cheering at football games on Saturday afternoon, worrying about surprise quizzes in Chem 3, scheming to get afternoon Coke dates with coeds. And here I was, lying in some woods with shells exploding all around me. That other life seemed like a dream, a lost, unbelievable paradise.

And then just as suddenly as it had started, the shelling stopped. I lay on the ground, holding my breath, waiting for the next one. It didn't come.

I lay stupefied, slow moving, slow thinking. That's what an intense bombardment does to you. It pounds the alertness out of you.

A call came over my radio from Colonel Rudd. Captain Sawyer had sent a runner to Colonel Rudd to report that another SIW (Self-Inflicted Wound) had shown up at battalion aid. This was the third one today. Three riflemen in the battalion had accidentally shot themselves in the foot. That's a lot of accidents.

Colonel Rudd was apoplectic. He immediately called up Captain O'Neill, the CO of George Company.

"We just got another SIW in from your company."

"I know about it," Captain O'Neill said darkly.

"Goddamn it, this has got to cease! What are you doing over there? Can't you keep your eye on your men?"

Captain O'Neill was the type of man who stands up for himself. I could sense the repressed anger in his voice.

"I can only be one place at a time. I can't stand over everybody every minute!"

"I want this yellow bastard court-martialed! I'm going to make an example out of him! I want you to check around and find some witnesses. Get their names and send that to me right away!"

"There are no witnesses. They wait till they're alone to do it. Do you think they're going to do it in front of anybody?"

I thought this was asking an awful lot of Captain O'Neill. Here he was pinned down in a perilous firefight, with machine guns firing at him and 88s raining down from overhead, and Colonel Rudd was asking him to put that aside and concentrate on a legal matter.

The SIWs couldn't stand the suspense of seeing whether they would be killed, wounded, or come out unscathed, so they unilaterally left the game, eliminated the risk factor, and took a relatively small loss. After the war, this guy would join the American Legion and limp through the Memorial Day parade, a war hero. He would say he stepped on a mine. Who would know the difference? Twenty years from now he would lean back in a soft chair in the fall and listen to the World Series. Not everybody would be able to do that.

There was a call for more ammo.

"Easy One to Kingfish Major. Over."

"Kingfish Major to Easy One. Over."

"Kingfish Major. We're running low on apples. Do you want me to send a couple of men back to pick some up? I don't really have anybody I can spare right now. Over."

"Easy One. No, no. You stay put. We'll have it brought up. Out."

Fox Company called for five more bathtubs.

That was a wasted call, I thought. There were more calls for bathtubs than there were wounded going back. The stretcher bearers were obviously behind on their pickups. What was the point in calling for more bathtubs when the bearers couldn't take care of the wounded that were already waiting for them?

I was having trouble with my right hand. It was because of my Army-issue wool-knit gloves. The tops of three middle fingers of my right-hand glove had been worn off. It left three fingertips exposed to the cold. The fingers were raw-red, swollen and they were paining me. I tried pulling the glove away from the wrist, up over the fingers, but that didn't help much. The cold still got in there.

I had joined the outfit with practically a brand-new pair of wool-knit gloves. One day I laid my gloves on the table and went down cellar to get some briquets. When I got back, somebody had taken my gloves and left these in their place. I was sick about it. It had to be somebody in communications who took them because there were only radio and wire guys in the house. At the repot depots I had been careful to keep the gloves on my person at all times, but I had trusted all the guys in communications. That was a mistake. I thought we were a family and family members don't steal from each other, or at least they didn't in my family. There was no way to tell who had done it. All the gloves looked alike.

(Later I went to our Supply Sergeant and asked him to get me a new pair of gloves. He said, "I could requisition them for you but they won't get here till July." So much for our unbelievably well-supplied Army. No winter gloves available in the wintertime. Or was the Supply Sergeant just too lazy to fill out a form? I don't know. I thought of taking a pair off a German prisoner, but Sergeant Drummond gave me food for thought. "I don't know if I would do that if I were you. If you're taken prisoner, and they see you wearing them, they might shoot you because of it." I didn't do it.)

After the heavy shelling, there was a seemingly long interval of nothing, and then an 88 came over. I threw myself face down and burrowed into the snow with all my might. It passed over me. Another one came. It veered off. The third one came. Its whistle got louder and louder and louder. *Oh, my God!* It was coming in on me!

They say that at a time like this your whole life flashes before your eyes. I don't know if it was because I had lived a fuller life than most but there was no time for my whole life to flash before my eyes. I only had time to scream silently, *Save me, Lord!* and it was in on me.

I did not hear the explosion; you have to be outside it to hear it. I was at the center of a tremendous force. I had the physical authority of a leaf in the wind. The air pressure blasted me with such power my body was anesthetized, cut off from me, my mind dulled. My spirit was floating above the earth.

I felt I was in the air but not that I had been tossed there. Rather, I felt that I was immobile and it was the earth that had fallen away from me.

And then it was over. I lay on the ground. I was in a stupor. I could not feel my body. I thought I was dying. Then my mind started to come back. My mind was able to think. That was a good sign. Maybe I wasn't dead.

My body was numb. I could not feel anything. I thought for sure I must be wounded. I looked for wounds and blood. I didn't see any. But my body wasn't sending me any signals. My hands could help. I started by squeezing my ankles to see what would happen. The ankles seemed all right. I worked my way up, squeezing my calves, knees, thighs, hips, ass, sides, shoulders, arms, neck, face. Everything was still numb but seemed whole.

Then I saw my helmet three feet away from me. I hadn't noticed I didn't have it on. I had had it tightly buckled under my chin and it had been blown off my head.

And there on the snow, directly in front of me, six inches from where my head had been lying, was a chunk of shrapnel the size of a baseball. I picked it up and hefted it. It was heavy. It had multi-jagged, razor-sharp edges.

I was alive when I could just as easily have been dead. I felt a surge of wild joy. I was in a state of sublime bliss.

That shell was beneficial to me. It calmed me down. It cleared my mind. I stopped thinking about college and my cousin in Portugal.

(That shell was a master teacher. I walked out of those woods a different person from the one who had walked in. I had never thought much about life and death. Now I knew something. I knew how precarious life is. And in my life as a civilian after the war, I had the usual bumpy ride of an ordinary human, vexations, conflicts, disappointments, failures, but those things never depressed me past a certain point because I knew they weren't important. What is really important is being alive. Every day of life, every hour, every minute, is a priceless gift to be enjoyed. That shell taught me that and I never forgot it.)

The afternoon dragged on. The stretcher bearers continued carrying their human cargo up the trail. I continued holding the receiver to my ear. The German shelling continued its on-again, off-again pacing.

The line companies had suffered significant losses. From the calls I sensed a growing concern over the possibility of a German counterattack. Were the line companies in a condition that would enable them to stop a counterattack?

The shadows lengthened. The shelling ceased. Darkness came. It was really dark, not like last night when the moon was out. The stretcher bearers made one last pickup in the dark and then they didn't return. I figured they had gotten everybody out.

The radio transmissions dwindled off. The men were digging in for the night. Nobody came down the trail and nobody went up it.

I was alone in the woods. I lay on my back, using the radio to prop up my head, and relaxed. I had nothing to do. All I had to do was wait for whatever was to happen. I did so without any impatience whatsoever. I guessed they had forgotten about me. I wasn't going to remind anybody I was out here. I was cold but there were worse places to be.

I looked at my wrist watch with the luminescent dial. It was eleven o'clock. In an hour it will be midnight, I thought, and I will have lived through my first day of combat. It had been some day, a day that seemed like a year. If today was a sample of days to come, then my prospects for survival looked pretty grim.

I heard footsteps.

It was Lieutenant Tidwell.

"Come on," he said. "We're going to set up an OP (Observation Post)."

I tried to get up. I was like a frozen log. It had been hours since I last stood up. I lurched stiffly after him.

We walked down to the river. The engineers had built a narrow footbridge over it. We started across. I heard voices underneath us. The engineers were still working on the bridge and were discussing what they were doing. I did not have an unobstructed view of them. I wondered what they were standing on. They couldn't have been in the water. They'd freeze to death.

The river was surprisingly wide. To cross it in a boat meant that you were under fire for a long time. It must have been hell.

A short distance from the river we came to a lone farmhouse. It was out here in the countryside all by itself. It was formidable, built like a fort. It had a courtyard with a high concrete wall going all the way around it. Of course, I couldn't see that in the dark. I saw it the next day in the daylight.

Lieutenant Tidwell and I entered the courtyard. There was an 88, a dud, lying by my feet. It didn't look so scary lying there. I stepped over it.

I heard voices coming from over by the wall. I looked but all I could see was shadowy forms in the dark. It was a strange chorus, each voice singing its own tune. Groans. Sudden incoherent calls in delirium. Cries of pain. And then a normal voice rising above the din,

"Keep quiet, you guys!" I guess he couldn't stand it anymore. They paid him no heed.

I estimated there were ten to twelve men in the chorus. And I realized with astonishment who they were. Wounded men placed together over by the wall. I had assumed the stretcher bearers got everybody. They hadn't.

Were the stretcher bearers taking a long break to eat and rest or had they knocked off for the night? If they had knocked off till daylight, it was going to be a long, long night for these men. Would the seriously wounded among them, if there were any, make it through the night out here in the freezing cold? Why hadn't all of these men at least been placed inside the farmhouse where they would have been sheltered from the elements?

Lieutenant Tidwell and I entered the farmhouse. We made our way inside the house with the aid of his flashlight. He selected a large room on the bottom floor and started vigorously pumping up a lamp he had brought. Once lit, it gave a terrific white light. A very good lamp indeed.

Then he called battalion CP on my radio and told Colonel Rudd the place was ready for him.

In about thirty minutes Colonel Rudd showed up with his radio operator, Harry Folenius. He had left all the other officers back at the CP. But it was kind of silly to call the OP the OP. Wherever Colonel Rudd was, that was the CP.

Ten minutes after that, an officer walked in with two wire men, Spumoni and Hillbilly. It was Lieutenant Spinner, the officer in charge of communications. I was under his command. I had never seen him before, nor he me. He gave me a quick, dismissive glance as he walked in. I knew he didn't know my name.

Lieutenant Spinner was a tall, angular fellow. His face had a peculiar, petulant look. I realized it was the way his lower lip stuck out. Irrationally the thought flashed across my mind—Mama's boy.

I couldn't take my eyes off his hands. He was wearing a magnificent pair of gloves. They were a resplendent bright yellow, supple, made of some kind of animal skin. The insides were lined with toasty-warm fur. The gloves weren't skimpy. They were extra long, came up almost to his elbows, and flared out at the end. They looked brand new. Somebody must have sent them from home. Other than girls, I had never envied anybody anything. But I envied Lieutenant Spinner his gloves with all my heart.

Lieutenant Spinner went behind the table and conferred quietly with Colonel Rudd. Then he came around and motioned for Spumoni and Hillbilly to follow him. As he passed me, he said, "You, too." The four of us trooped out.

Spumoni and Hillbilly had left a wheel of wire outside the OP. There was an iron bar going through the center of the wheel. Spumoni and Hillbilly picked up the wheel by the bar, one man on each side of the wheel, and they proceeded to lay out wire as they followed Lieutenant Spinner. I brought up the rear.

We were walking away from the river.

We didn't go very far when Lieutenant Spinner stopped.

"Wait here," he told us.

I could hear voices on my left. It sounded like guys spread out, calling to each other. I presumed they were dug in, although I didn't know how they could dig up this frozen ground.

Lieutenant Spinner went over to the nearest guy. I heard him talking to the guy but I couldn't make out what he was saying. After a while he came back.

"The password for tonight is *Green*," he said to us, "and the counter is *Hornet*. Be sure you remember them. If we get separated and you forget them, you could get shot."

That was an effective way to put it. I was sure I wasn't going to forget them.

We walked away, keeping to the right of the men who had been calling to each other. Everything was quiet. Then one of the men we had just left fired his rifle. The shot triggered a mass reaction. The whole company fired their rifles. It was a furious volley but it only lasted ten seconds. Then everything was quiet again.

Had somebody been spooked and ignited everyone's fears? In the dark had one man heard imaginary sounds from an unseen enemy?

We continued on our way. We were in gently rolling country. Nobody had been here. The crust of the snow was smooth and unbroken. The wind had blown the snow into drifts. We had to fight our way through them, sinking down in the snow up to our waists. The snow was ass-deep on a tall Indian, as they say.

We floundered through the snow, our movements slow and ponderous. I was having a helluva hard time carrying my radio. It was because of the broken strap. Held by only the one strap, the radio swung erratically on my back. I tried putting my right arm behind me to hold the radio against my back but that didn't work. So I ended up carrying the radio under my right arm. It was an awkward burden and it threw me off balance. If the radio had had two straps like it was supposed to, it would have fit snugly against my back and I would have had two arms free. I cursed Sergeant Drummond for having given me this radio.

In addition, my carbine, which I had slung, kept slipping off my left shoulder. And my overshoes were not a proper fit. They were too big. Once my feet sank into the snow, it required real effort to pull them out. The overshoes left enormous footprints. You would have thought I was a giant.

But I could see that Spumoni and Hillbilly were having their troubles, too. Not only were they carrying the heavy wheel of wire, but they had to lay out wire at the same time. They each had a rifle slung on their left shoulder.

The only one in good shape was Lieutenant Spinner. He carried nothing. He had both arms free. Well, he carried a .45 in a hip holster but that didn't slow him down any. And he had long skinny legs, perfect for snow.

Lieutenant Spinner stopped to rest. We stood together, all breathing heavily. Nobody said anything. We didn't have the breath to talk even if we had something to say, which nobody did. Then we set off again, in the same order, Lieutenant Spinner in front, Spumoni and Hillbilly next, me last.

This was scarier than hell. What were we doing out here all by ourselves? Where were we going? What were we supposed to do? I had no idea. Nobody ever told me anything. Were we in what used to be called No Man's Land in the First World War?

Lieutenant Spinner was head of communications, Spumoni and Hillbilly were wire men, and I was a radio man. It must have something to do with communications, but what? Were we going to set up a communications link out here in the open? But why? We had excellent radio reception right now between the line companies and battalion CP. Colonel Rudd had set up an OP on this side of the river because he wanted to be closer to the action, not because there was any communication need for it. And the OP was so close to the line companies, radio reception between the two would be loud and clear. So what were we doing out here? Who were we going to communicate with? But whatever we were doing, wherever we were going, it didn't feel right.

Suddenly the moon came out from behind the clouds. It was like broad daylight. How nice, I thought. Now I can see things. Then I got a second thought. No, it's not so nice. If I can see things, the Germans can see us. Was someone behind a machine gun right now watching us approach like ducks in a row?

We were out in the open. We could be picked off from a great distance. Our dark overcoats against the white background of snow made us perfect targets. How could they miss? Why weren't we issued snow uniforms? If you're going to fight in the snow, you should have a snow uniform. I noticed that several infantrymen going down the trail had tried to improvise with homemade snow uniforms. They had taken a white bedsheet, cut a hole in it for their head, and tried to drape it around their body, but it didn't look like it would hold up.

Running parallel with us off to our right were some woods. These woods were low, thick, impenetrable, black, forbidding, as still as death. Every time I looked, the woods seemed to be getting closer. We weren't walking toward them so that had to be an illusion. But they seemed alive and they seemed to be advancing on us. Were there Germans in those woods?

What if we blundered into the German lines? I kept expecting a German patrol to pop up in front of us. They would be in a semicircle, their weapons pointed at us. Would they take us prisoners? Or worse, would they shoot us on the spot?

We came to a steep incline. It had no snow on it, just ice. There was no way I could keep my footing going up it. I went down to my hands and knees and crawled. Barbed wire was strung straight up the incline. I grasped the barbed wire, being careful to seize it between the barbs, and pulled myself to the top.

We kept on.

We came to a gentle rise. Lieutenant Spinner stopped at the top of it.

"Give me your receiver," he said curtly to me.

I handed it to him.

He turned his back to us and talked softly into the receiver. I could not hear what he was saying.

Suddenly he turned around and half-handed, half-tossed the receiver to me.

"Let's get out of here!" he cried.

His eyes were wild with fear and his voice was pure panic. It had to be a German counterattack. What else could produce an effect like that?

He took off like a bat out of hell and I was right on his heels. A dog will chase almost anything that moves fast in front of him and maybe that instinct is in humans, too. Spumoni and Hillbilly had to take time to cut the wire so now they were bringing up the rear. They still carried the wheel of wire and I still carried my radio.

Lieutenant Spinner plunged through the snow like a man possessed. He wasn't stopping and he wasn't looking back. In fact, he never did look back.

I was trying to keep up but he started pulling away from me. I was in a panic. He was going back a different way than we had come. I recognized nothing in the landscape. I was lost. And I had a very poor sense of direction. Left to myself, it was a fifty-fifty chance as to which line I would end up at, German or American. And I didn't know if Spumoni and Hillbilly knew the way back and I wasn't going to wait around to find out. Lieutenant Spinner seemed to know where he was going. I had to keep him in sight no matter what.

He was getting away from me. I desperately tried to increase my speed. I thought of chucking my radio. Carrying the goddamn thing under my arm was what was slowing me down. But if I did and we got back, I knew there would be hell to pay, maybe they'd even send me to a rifle company, so I hung on to it.

I heard Hillbilly's frantic cry behind me.

"Wait for us! Wait for us!"

Tough shit, Hillbilly. It was every man for himself. I could see that was how the game was played out here. Like Lieutenant Spinner, I wasn't about to look back.

I had run track in high school, the distance runs, and I was a mediocre runner probably because I couldn't push my body past a certain point in accepting pain. Now, chasing Spinner, I went past that point. I dissociated myself from my body. Whatever it was feeling could not affect my frenzy of determination to keep him in sight.

I started down a hill. I broke into a run, figuring that momentum would take me to the bottom quickly and thus make up some of the ground I had lost in my pursuit of Spinner. There was only six inches of snow on the hill but there was ice underneath the snow. My feet slipped and I fell down hard on my side, ramming the radio against my ribs. I didn't have time to feel pain. I scrambled to my feet and hurtled forward. My legs shot out from under me and I fell on my back. I slid a surprisingly long distance. When I came to a stop, I struggled to my feet and did my best not to do what my lungs were screaming for me to do, which was to slow down.

Lieutenant Spinner stopped on the road outside the OP. I staggered up to him. Another ten feet and I couldn't have made it. I doubled over. I couldn't breathe. My mouth was wide open and I gasped for oxygen.

Spumoni and Hillbilly came up. I heard Spumoni's noisy death rattle. He was packing a little extra weight around his middle so I guess that didn't help. He looked like he was about to keel over with a heart attack.

Gradually, slowly, we recovered. I was able to stand up straight and look normal.

"You two guys find Henderson and help him," Lieutenant Spinner said to Spumoni and Hillbilly. They went off, carrying the wheel of wire between them.

"You come on with me," Lieutenant Spinner said to me.

We entered the courtyard.

The wounded were still there but they were quieter.

We went in the OP. Colonel Rudd didn't say a word to Lieutenant Spinner when we walked in. He hardly looked at him. Lieutenant Spinner sat down in a chair at the table and I sat next to Harry Folenius. Lieutenant Tidwell was still there at the table. Two other officers I didn't know had come while we were gone and were asleep on the floor under their blankets.

After about fifteen minutes, Colonel Rudd said, "Spinner, you better get out there and work on the lines."

Lieutenant Spinner didn't look like he was too happy to go out but he got up and left.

I felt sorry for him and the wire men. They were out there in the cold and dark, looking for breaks in the lines and it was all a waste of time. They would find a break and repair it but there would be two or three other breaks in the same line. It was the 88s. They blew the lines apart. In the whole three-day engagement we had a total of about ten minutes of phone communication with the line companies. We communicated exclusively by radio. The linemen were out there night and day searching for breaks. But it was all for nothing.

"I'm going back to the CP," Harry Folenius said to me. "You take over here."

That meant I would be Colonel Rudd's operator. That made me more than a little nervous. I didn't want to fuck up with him. I put my receiver to my ear and listened intently. Folenius then left, taking his radio with him.

"O'Neill has been complaining about the new fellows," Colonel Rudd said morosely to Lieutenant Tidwell. "They keep their heads down and won't look up. They think that if they just lie there and don't look up, the Krauts can't see them. They're getting killed without firing a shot."

It was now four o'clock in the morning.

Lieutenant Spinner came back in. He looked exhausted.

"The lines are in," he said.

He pulled his gloves off and unrolled a sleeping bag on the floor. The bag had thick insulation. This guy travels first class, I thought. He took off his helmet and overshoes and got in the bag and was asleep before he was horizontal.

About fifteen minutes after Lieutenant Spinner had fallen asleep, Colonel Rudd said to Lieutenant Tidwell, "I think I'll call Jerry Schumacher at Regiment."

There was a working phone line in from battalion CP back to Regiment, but to make that connection he had to reach the switchboard in the cellar of the CP.

He picked up the phone and turned the crank on the leather case.

Moura, the switchboard operator, didn't answer. The line was dead.

"Goddamn it!"

He went over to Lieutenant Spinner and bent over him.

"Spinner! Wake up!" he yelled.

The lieutenant did not respond.

Colonel Rudd grabbed him by the shoulder and shook him roughly.

Spinner sat up in his sleeping bag.

"Huh?" he said.

He wasn't awake yet.

"Spinner, get out there and fix those goddamn lines!"

Lieutenant Spinner just stared at him, his mouth open.

Then the strangest thing happened. Sitting there in his sleeping bag, Spinner began to cry. The floodgates opened and the tears poured down his cheeks. This was no ordinary cry. Great heaving convulsive sobs shook his body. He tried to talk but could not get any words out.

"Get a hold of yourself, man," Colonel Rudd growled.

Lieutenant Tidwell and I looked away. We didn't want to add to Spinner's embarrassment by staring at him.

Spinner's nose was running. He took the back of his hand and rubbed it across his nostrils.

He kept on crying. He was really out of control. Finally the sobs began to decrease in intensity and he gradually quieted. He put on his helmet and overshoes and left without a word.

I didn't think any the less of Lieutenant Spinner for having cried. It was just one of those things. The man had been pushed beyond the limits of his endurance and lost control of himself. That was all it was. I suppose that according to the manly code, he should have been ashamed of himself for crying. But not being manly myself, I didn't see it that way.

Groton, another radio operator, came over to the OP and relieved me at about two o'clock that afternoon.

I was glad to be relieved. I hadn't eaten anything since the midnight breakfast. I hadn't slept since the night before the midnight breakfast. I was ready to be relieved.

6

Jelich

IT WAS WEIRD. The guy I hit it off best with was the oldest guy in the outfit, not including officers. It was Jelich. He was thirty years old, medium height, lean and wiry, sharp-nosed, unmarried. He was a jeep driver and a helluva good driver. I found that out one dark night when we were going down a narrow country road. But first we had gone down the road in the daylight of the afternoon. We had been warned, "Stay on the road. The shoulders are mined." There had been no time to sweep the shoulders with metal detectors.

Jelich, Colonel Rudd, and I were in the jeep. And we soon saw why the warning had gone out. A 2 1/2 ton truck had been coming west when it met another 2 1/2 ton truck going east, as we were. The guy going west was courteous and his courtesy cost him his life. He pulled partly off the road to let the other guy by and he drove onto a mine. It blew him out of the cab and blew one of his tires as high as a nearby tall tree. The tire hung there on an uppermost branch like an ornament on a Christmas tree. We saw the wreck and the tire as we drove by.

We dropped Colonel Rudd off at Easy Company's CP, retraced our route back to battalion CP, and that night were summoned forward again by Colonel Rudd. We had to go back down the road, this time in pitch blackness, with our headlights off. I looked out of the jeep and all I could see was black ink. How could Jelich see to drive? He drove with complete focus on his task but all the while he was as cool as a cucumber. I was sweating. I kept seeing that tire in the tree and thinking I might join it at any moment. We didn't say a word as he drove. And, obviously, we made it.

I became acquainted with Jelich that first week when we were all laying around, waiting to cross the Sauer. We had plenty of time to talk then. I can remember the first words I ever heard him say.

He said, "Those guys back at Regiment are wearing so many medals they have to go through doors sideways."

Nobody wears medals that extend out from your chest. It was a nonsensical statement but I found it irresistibly funny. And that's always a good beginning to a friendship, because I value anybody who can make me laugh.

"How long have you been overseas?" Jelich asked me that first day.

"Six weeks," I said.

"I've been overseas three years," he said.

"Wow! I didn't know anybody had been overseas that long."

"Oh, yeah. We went to Iceland in March of 1942."

"I didn't know we had any troops in Iceland."

"Oh, yeah. We were there a year and a half."

"Why did they send you there?"

"I think they were afraid the Krauts were going to take it so we beat them to the punch."

"That's interesting."

"Iceland was like being at the North Pole. A goddamn bleak rock. The winds blow you off your feet. And it seems like either snow or rain or sleet is always whipping you across the face. And in the wintertime you get three hours of daylight. It's a cold, miserable place."

"How'd you get along with the people?"

"Those fish heads up there wouldn't have anything to do with us. They wouldn't talk to us. I guess they thought we wanted to rape their daughters. But they didn't talk to each other either. A climate like that, it does things to you. All we could do was sit by our little stove in the hut and listen to the wind howling outside.

"We were sure glad to get out of that place. When we got on the boat, everybody was real happy. We all thought we were going home. Instead they took us to England and then they sent us to Ireland to train for the invasion.

"When we were in Ireland, we were in these barracks. And somebody found an Irish country girl and smuggled her into the barracks. And then she proceeded to fuck everybody in the barracks. It was the most amazing thing."

"You, too?"

"No, no, no. Not me. I don't go for mob scenes. It's a good thing she didn't have the clap. She would have put the whole barracks on sick call.

"She was in that barracks for three days. They used to smuggle in food to her from the mess hall. I don't know why she did it. I could see it if she was charging them but she did it free. No money exchanged hands. And she didn't seem to particularly enjoy it. The guys told me she just lay there like a sack of beans. She used to drive the guys crazy. Right in the middle of it, she'd say to a guy, 'Do you have any gum?' or 'Do you have a cigarette?' They'd say, 'Goddamn it! Can't you wait till I'm through?'

"I hated to go in the barracks. You'd open the door and the smell of stale fuck would hit you in the face. The place stunk. And all night long you'd hear guys going, 'Aaaaahhh!' She took on all comers, no questions asked. And lots of guys more than once. It seemed like every time I looked, Groton was up on her. 'I never pass up free ass,' he told me.

"Finally, after three days, the guys started getting nervous about it. What if one of the officers pulled a surprise inspection and found her in there? So they decided they had to get rid of her. But here's the funny part. When they told her she had to go, she got mad as hell. She started swearing at them. She didn't want to go. They tried to bribe her with packs of cigarettes and gum but she still wouldn't go. Finally, they actually had to grab her and give her the bum's rush out the door.

"I've got to take a piss," Jelich said. When he got back, he said to me, "You're lucky you came when you did. If you had come earlier, you might have been here for Metz. And let me tell you something, no matter how bad things might get from here on out, they won't be half as bad as Metz was."

"Is that a town?"

"No. It's a fort with tunnels. We had to go into those tunnels. How would you like to go into a tunnel about a yard wide and so dark you can't see your hand in front of your face? They say Patton is a genius but I don't know. They call him Old Blood and Guts. We have a saying, 'His guts and our blood.' Why he sent us in there, I've never been able to figure out. We couldn't use our planes, we couldn't use our tanks, we couldn't use our artillery. The advantage was all with the Krauts. They knew those tunnels like they knew the backs of their hands and we didn't. We were lost in there. They'd sneak up behind us and throw grenades at us.

"I'm no general but I often thought, Why go in there and meet them head-on? Why not go around them? They're sitting in a fort. They're not going anywhere. Wait them out. If you go in after them, the losses are mostly going to be on your side, and that's exactly what happened. But if you wait for them to come out, then the losses are going to be on their side.

"The air in the tunnels was real bad. It was full of dust and fumes. You couldn't breathe in there. There was no ventilation. There'd be a big steel door blocking your way, so the engineers would come up and set a demolition charge. Well, after the explosion, there'd be all these gases. I think there was a lot of carbon monoxide. Guys were passing out.

"You'd go into a tunnel and the Krauts would have a machine gun set up at the other end. How could they miss? Sometimes they were so close to you, you could hear them talking.

"And there was something nobody knew about. The Krauts at the fort were not ordinary Krauts. They were running an OCS (Officer Candidate School) right there at Metz. They had gone through the whole German Army and hand-picked the best noncoms and sent them to Metz to make officers out of them. And these were the guys we were up against. They were all experienced combat veterans. They were tough, tough fighters. And they were all trying to outdo each other, to impress their officers. We never came across a bunch like them before or since.

"When the brass finally realized it wasn't going to work, they pulled us out. But we took a helluva beating in there, lost a lot of guys. I don't think there's hardly any guys left in the rifle companies who were at Metz.

"After Metz we got a lot of replacements. Then we went through some really bad weather. It rained day after day and it turned cold. We were living in the mud. Quite a few guys got trench foot. This was before we got our overshoes. My best friend got it. We had been together since we trained in Louisiana in '41. The lucky son of a gun. He's back in the States now in a hospital. And I'm still here."

"I've heard of trench foot," I said. "But I don't really know much about it. How do you get it?"

"Well, if your feet are wet and cold day after day, you can get it. And that's what happened to us. Our shoes were water-logged. And what happens I think is this. The blood doesn't circulate to your feet. So I think part of the foot or the whole foot starts to die. Your feet swell up. And it can turn to gangrene. Sometimes they have to amputate."

(In a period of two weeks, November 2–16, 1944, the 28th Division reported 750 cases of trench foot. The men had not been issued rubber overshoes. The generals had not learned one of the lessons of World War I.)

About a month after this conversation with Jelich, my feet began to itch. This was no minor thing. It got worse and worse. Both my feet were on fire with the itching and it got to a point where it was driving me wild. I took to stamping my boots on the ground and smashing one boot against the other in the hope that the sensation of pain would deaden my feet to the itching. But relief was only momentary.

I didn't know what to do. It was like a toothache. I couldn't get away from it for even a minute. Then a thought flashed through my mind. Did I have trench foot? Jelich had not mentioned itching as a symptom of trench foot and I did not believe that my feet had swelled up. Still, something obviously was going on with my feet. Could it be the first stages of trench foot? Could I be that lucky? The possibility buoyed me up and made my suffering almost desirable.

Certainly it was worth a shot. And even if I didn't have trench foot, I wanted the itching to be treated. It was more than a person could stand. It was driving me out of my mind. So I went to see Captain Sawyer at battalion aid.

I was the only man in there except for the aid men, who were hanging around, listening to me talk to Captain Sawyer.

I described the itching to Captain Sawyer, who heard me out with bored indifference. I was very careful not to mention the words *trench foot*. That would have killed it on the spot. He would have read my mind. I expected him to tell me to take off my boots so he could examine my feet, but he did not do so. I rightly took this to be a bad sign.

"Wash your feet every night," he said with a straight face and walked away, leaving me standing there like a fool with my mouth open.

Was this his idea of a joke, a little bit of medical humor, designed to break up the tedium of a quiet afternoon for the aid men? There was no way on earth I could wash my feet every night and he knew it. The only water available to us was a small amount of drinking water we toted around in a can in our trailer. There was no water for feet.

Apparently my feet, acting independently of me, took note of Captain Sawyer's dismissal, realized the situation was hopeless, and accepted defeat, for the very next day they began to itch less and gradually over the next couple of days returned to a normal state.

7

Nobody Gets Out

I WAS SITTING in the back seat of a jeep with my radio. The jeep was parked alongside the road in a small turnout. Colonel Rudd and Jelich were at battalion CP. I was waiting for them to come back.

There was a dead German soldier sprawled out on the road a few feet from me. He was lying front down with his head turned sideways. The top of his head was missing. You could see right down into his head. It was like an eggshell with one end open. Despite that, I could see he had long blond hair. It was matted with blood.

A Sherman tank came clattering down the dirt road in a big hurry. One of its tracks went right over the dead German's head. It wasn't as if the driver had deliberately run him over. He had no choice. The road was narrow and he was further hemmed in by piles of rubble on both sides.

Now the dead soldier's face was mush. His features were gone. If his mother could see him now, would she still scream with ecstasy when Hitler drove slowly by in that open car, standing in the front with that smirk on his face? And if they could have shown this soldier's face on German newsreels in 1939 instead of the victorious warriors smiling and strutting across Poland, would it have made a difference?

It was strange about the dead. Nobody was in a hurry to pick up the German dead. They lay where they fell and everybody went about their business unconcerned. They became part of the scenery. I suppose it was good psychology not to pick them up. We could all see then that they were not supermen. In fact, it was comforting to see a dead German. One less guy to try to kill you.

But it was a different story with the American dead. They were whisked out of sight as quickly as possible. I suppose that was good psychology, too. You didn't want live American soldiers looking at dead American soldiers because it brought to mind what could happen at any time. I went by a Sherman tank once. It had been knocked out by a Tiger Royal, a very common occurrence with our inferior tanks. The Sherman was still smoking. I was there ten minutes after it had been hit. There were two tank men face down in the dirt a few feet from the tank. And there was one guy bent over the turret hatch, half in and half out of the tank. I came back about half an hour later and somebody had draped G.I. blankets over the three bodies. Then I went forward again in a little while and now the bodies were gone.

A company of infantrymen came marching single file down the road, moving forward into the line. It was not a destination that inspired lighthearted conversation. They were silent and stony-faced. Where, oh where, was that tiresome fellow from Brooklyn, wisecracking his way down the road into danger, beloved by Hollywood, a fixture in every war movie? The infantrymen were on the opposite side of the road. One of them broke away from the column and started running across the road toward my jeep. It took me a moment to recognize him. It was Berseglaria. I hadn't seen him since that day in the courtyard when we were replacements.

He stuck his head in the jeep.

"Charley," he said, "can you get me out of here?"

His voice and face were intense, desperate, pleading.

"I'll do what I can," I lied. "If we ever need another operator, I'll tell the sergeant about you."

"Thanks, Charley. Thanks! Thanks!"

He turned and started running to get back to his place in line.

I suddenly remembered.

"Do you ever see Browny?" I called after him.

He turned and yelled over his shoulder.

"He got his leg blown off the first day!"

And he was gone.

Poor Berseglaria. He was fucked and didn't know it. Nobody gets out of a rifle company. It's a door that only opens one way, in. You leave when they carry you out, if you're unlucky, dead, or if you're lucky, wounded. But nobody just walks away. That was the unwritten law. I had no power to get Berseglaria out. My sergeant had no power to get him out.

In this instance I thought the Army was right. If one man was allowed to escape, what would happen to the morale of the men left behind? Being a foot soldier was so horrible that the only way a man could stand it was if he felt there was no way out. Then he accepted his fate and took his chances. But if he thought escape was possible, it would drive him nuts.

We had one guy, a jeep driver working out of battalion. I had been told about him and one day I saw for myself what they were talking about. He and I were driving down a road when all of a sudden an 88 came whistling down on us. He immediately jammed on the brakes and I dove for the ground.

He had killed the engine but he didn't move from behind the wheel. He stayed there, slumped over, shaking violently, drooling, his teeth chattering, his eyes rolling around in his head. And long after the danger had passed, he remained that way, slumped over, shaking violently, totally unable to function. He was perfectly normal until an 88 came anywhere near him, and then he went into that kind of a fit. I left him there and walked away, because people were waiting for me and my radio.

He was a danger to himself because he was at greater risk from flying shrapnel sitting in a jeep than he would have been flat on the ground.

His unreliability caused the battalion to use him as a driver only when they were desperate. They used him mostly for odd jobs on foot, running errands, delivering messages, stuff like that. He had no business being at the front, but there he was, and there he stayed. The point is, they refused to send him back to the rear where he belonged. He was like a walking message for everybody—"Forget about it. You're not getting out."

One day I was on duty at battalion CP. Word had just come down that the battalion was being relieved so all the officers were in a good mood, relaxed, the tension off.

The door suddenly opened and in marched a soldier. He was a little guy with thick glasses. I did a double take. It was like looking at my twin. His helmet seemed too big for his head.

The officers were all sitting behind a long table, like in *The Last Supper*, and there was Colonel Rudd, like Christ at the center. The officers were facing the door so they all looked up when the soldier came in. He knew where he was going. He marched stiffly to a spot in front of Colonel Rudd, keeping a respectful distance away, and came to a picture-perfect stop, his right heel smacking smartly against his left heel, and then he threw Colonel Rudd a beautiful salute.

Everybody's mouth fell open. Nobody saluted at the front. That was one of the things I liked about the front. I suppose it was because the officers didn't want it. If we were under enemy observation, and the enemy saw an individual being saluted, it would identify that person as an officer and he would become a prime target.

"Sir, Private Henry Gershon, Company G, requests permission to speak to the battalion commander!" he announced in ringing tones.

Colonel Rudd studied him. I think he was thinking: Who the hell is this guy?

"Permission granted," the colonel said.

"Sir, I have the permission of my company commander to speak to you."

Rudd nodded.

"Sir, I read in *Stars and Stripes* of a new program for enlisted men with combat experience. There's a shortage of second lieutenants, so outstanding infantrymen will be sent to the rear for an intensive six-week training course, and if they pass, they will be commissioned as second lieutenants in the infantry. I'd like to apply for this program."

"This is the first I've heard of this. But I'll certainly look into it."

"Thank you, sir."

"Do you consider yourself an outstanding infantryman?"

Private Gershon hesitated just a flick.

"Yes, sir. I think I am."

Rudd nodded.

"How long have you been with Company G?"

That hesitation again.

"Two weeks, sir."

Rudd nodded.

I had to give Rudd credit. He had teeth and he was quick to use them, but on this occasion he was unusually restrained, even gentle.

"It's rough, isn't it?"

"Yes, sir. It is."

"Of course, you understand, these things have to go through channels. They have to go through Regiment and then Division and then Army Headquarters. It can take a long, long time."

"Yes, sir. I understand."

"All right, I'll look into it," Rudd said curtly, dismissing him.

"Thank you, sir. Thank you for your consideration."

Private Gershon gave Rudd another great salute, did a perfect about-face, and marched out.

There wasn't a sound in the CP, and then just about the time Private Gershon got to the street, the room erupted into spontaneous laughter. Everybody was laughing. Nobody said anything. It was just understood.

The only way you're going to become a second lieutenant, Private Gershon, is if every officer in your company is killed or grievously wounded, and the same with the sergeants, and you lead what remains of your company in a counterattack and you personally capture forty-five Germans. Then they'll give you a battlefield commission. Other than that, forget it. But what good would that gold bar do you? There's no percentage to it. You'll still be in a rifle company and the 88s fall indiscriminately on second lieutenants and privates and all the ranks in between.

But Private Gershon didn't want to be an officer anyway. What he really wanted was to get the hell out of here.

Why had Captain O'Neill given him permission to speak to Colonel Rudd? Because Captain O'Neill liked his little joke. The officers of George Company were probably at their CP laughing right now.

Afterwards, Colonel Rudd summed it up the best. "There's a boy who wants to be away from here. Well, I guess we all would, at that," he said reflectively. It was the only time I ever heard him express that feeling.

8

"Ich Spreche Deutsch ein Wenig"

I SPOKE A LITTLE GERMAN from the semester I had had of it in college and it sure came in handy.

There weren't a lot of guys hanging around the house, just Jelich and Harry Folenius. So I decided to give them and myself a treat.

I looked for a likely farmhouse. That was no problem. Every house in town was a farmhouse. The farmhouses in the U.S. were out in the country, each one isolated. But the German farmhouses were side by side in town. The farmers walked to their fields.

I saw a Powerful Katrinka in her barnyard. There were chickens running around and she had one milk cow. I went over to her.

She must have weighed three hundred pounds. Her upper arms were as big around as my thighs, and her thighs were as big around as my trunk. But I knew from previous dealings with powerfully built farm wives, there was a good chance that within that massive body there beat the romantic heart of Woman Eternal.

"Haben Sie Eier?" I asked her.

"Nein. Keine Eier," she said quickly, shaking her head.

They always said that.

Whereupon I pulled out of my pocket a necklace. I didn't just pull it out. I artfully displayed it for her admiration, using both my hands, like a Fifth Avenue jewelry salesman. It's all in the presentation.

"Schön, nicht wahr?" I said.

Bingo. Her eyes sparkled and they didn't waver from the necklace.

The first thing I did when we stayed at a house was look for jewelry. If there was any, I confiscated it. Trinkets, baubles, bright glass, necklaces, earrings, bracelets, whatever I could find. They came in handy for just such an occasion as today.

Her eyes narrowed.

"Wieviele Eier?"

"Sechs," I said, holding up six fingers. That would give us two eggs apiece.

She disappeared into the house and came back with the eggs. I handed over the necklace.

"Danke schön," I said.

I very carefully carried the eggs back to our house. I cushioned them in my pockets with handkerchiefs and gloves.

Jelich and Folenius were elated when they saw the eggs.

"Hot dawg!" Folenius said.

Jelich was the cook and waiter. He quickly fried them, sunny side up, giving me my two over lightly.

All we got from the kitchen were powdered eggs so this was a treat. I did this fairly often when it was possible to do so and when there weren't too many guys around.

When the officers found out I knew a little German, they gave me an additional assignment. The officer in charge would pick out the nicest house in town for the battalion CP. My job was to run the Germans off. I used a little set spiel, my *"Sie haben halbe Stunde"* speech. "You have half an hour to get your belongings out of the house. Take whatever you want but you have only half an hour."

Then I watched them dash around like crazy, filling their cart with a mattress, blankets, pans, clothing, and various other household objects. Then the husband got behind the bar in the front of the cart and the wife went behind the cart and they both pushed it to some other house.

I noticed that Jelich had been down lately. Withdrawn. Morose. I figured the war was getting to him.

He sought me out for a private conversation.

"Do you think you could get me a bottle of schnapps?" he asked.

"I don't know. I can try," I said.

"Okay. I'll go with you."

"Sure."

We went.

An angular, raw-boned woman was in her barnyard. She looked hard-bitten.

I approached her.

"Haben Sie Schnaps?"

"Nein. Keinen Schnaps," she said, shaking her head.

I pulled out one of my prizes, a pretty brooch, a pair of butterflies on the wing. She snorted scornfully. This was going to be a hard sell. Sometimes they held out for a double. So I set the brooch aside and brought out a nifty pair of earrings. She dismissed them with a decisive gesture, a disdainful wave of the back of the hand.

"She's not going for it," I told Jelich. "I think you better forget about it."

"Ask her what she needs."

"Was brauchen Sie?"

"Ich brauche Seife."

"She says she needs soap."

"Ask her if you get her some soap, will she give you a bottle of schnapps?"

"Where are you going to get some soap?"

"Never mind. Just ask her."

I did.

She nodded affirmatively.

"Tell her we'll be right back."

I did.

Off we went. He was walking with purpose.

"Where are we going?"

"To the kitchen. One of the cooks is a friend of mine. I think I can get some soap off him."

That was a surprise. I didn't think the cooks had any friends. I thought they hated us all.

When we got a couple of houses from the kitchen, he said, "You wait here. I want to go in alone."

"Okay," I said.

Soon he was back.

"Did you get any?"

"Darn right I did," he said with a smile. He showed me under his coat. He was carrying a brand-new slab of harsh, yellow G.I. soap. We used it back in the States to launder clothes and to sterilize our mess gear, dipping the mess gear in a garbage can of soapy water and then rinsing the soap off.

We made the trade and then we went back to our house. Jelich took the bottle of schnapps from underneath his coat and hid it in his bedroll. I never saw it again. Not that I minded. I didn't want any of it. I'm not a drinker. But it surprised me. That wasn't like Jelich, to sneak drinks when nobody was looking.

9

The Assault Platoon

I WAS LOUNGING AROUND our house, reading *Stars and Stripes*.
Everybody else had gone.

The door opened and Lieutenant Spinner stuck his head in.

"I've been looking for you, Felix," he said. "Come out to the
trailer."

I put on my helmet and overcoat and went out.

This was rather unusual to have face-to-face contact with Lieutenant Spinner. Whenever he wanted one of us to do something, he
told Sergeant Drummond and Drummond told us. I guessed Drummond wasn't around this time.

Lieutenant Spinner was waiting by the radio trailer. He lifted up
the end of the tarpaulin and pulled out a radio. He rested it against
the tarpaulin.

"Take this radio to Captain O'Neill over at George Company.
He's short a radio and I told him I'd lend him one of ours."

I pulled the straps apart and slipped them on. The radio was nice
and snug against my back.

"Where will he be?"

"At their CP. He's waiting for it so don't dilly-dally."

"No, sir."

George Company was down the street a ways. I set out for their CP. I didn't like taking this radio to them. I didn't want to get anywhere near a rifle company. The stink of death was on them. It was like going into a ward of badly diseased patients. It was just bad luck to get within their orbit.

I found the wooden sign:

Co. G

CP

There were a lot of guys milling around outside. Something was going on. I went in the house.

Captain O'Neill was sitting at a table. His radio operator was sitting next to him.

I swung the radio off my back and laid it on the table.

"Here you are, sir," I said cheerily, "the radio that Lieutenant Spinner promised you."

He looked at me sourly.

Not ever a word of thanks. That's how the officers were.

I turned to go when he said coldly, "I didn't ask for a radio. I asked for an operator and a radio."

I caught my breath. A trap door was opening beneath my feet.

"I don't know anything about that, sir," I said firmly. "All Lieutenant Spinner asked me to do was bring you a radio."

"It was understood between us. A radio and an operator."

"That's not what he told me," I insisted.

"I asked for a radio and an operator."

"That's not what he told me," I repeated desperately.

Captain O'Neill was getting exasperated with the conversation.

He grabbed the receiver of his phone and extended it to me.

"Here. Call him up."

I badly wanted to, to straighten out this mess, but I thought fast. If I embarrassed Spinner in front of other officers by questioning him, I would get it up the ass for sure. It was a battle I could not win, and worse, by being obstreperous, I could play this into a permanent assignment with a rifle company. You can't question an officer's authority. He will show you who's boss.

I didn't take the proffered phone.

"No. That's all right, Captain," I said grimly. I was getting fucked and my angry eyes showed I knew it.

I put the radio on my back.

"Report to Lieutenant Laurie," Captain O'Neill said. "He's leading the assault platoon."

Assault platoon. Could two words more chilling than those exist in the English language? My blood drained away. I felt like I was going to faint. This was a nightmare but I wasn't dreaming it. Bad enough that I was going with a rifle company, but an *assault platoon!* Things were getting worse by the minute. Five minutes ago I was delivering a radio. And now I was part of an assault platoon. So that was how death came upon you, when you were least expecting it.

I went outside in a daze.

I went up to a soldier.

"Where is Lieutenant Laurie?"

"That's him over there," he said pointing.

I went over to him.

"I'm your radio operator, sir," I said.

"Good," he said and gave me a big friendly smile.

Lieutenant Laurie was new to the company, a replacement officer. He was a recent VMI graduate, a newly minted second lieutenant, cannon fodder if there ever was any. Under his helmet he had short blond hair. He had crystal-clear blue eyes. He was young for an officer, my age. But he looked even younger than that. He looked like he was about eighteen. He didn't look like he shaved.

"All right! Let's go!" he commanded.

And off we went.

He was in front, leading the single-file column, and I was right behind him. I walked with a heavy heart, as did all the men behind me. I didn't need to take my cue from them. But if I had thought otherwise, all I needed to do was look at them, as silent and grim as men walking to their execution, and I would have known that what lay ahead was not good. They knew that much better than I did.

On the other hand, Lieutenant Laurie did not walk with a heavy heart. His step was light, jaunty even. He might have been going for a walk in the park. He looked like he might break out whistling. I thought sickeningly, "This kid has no idea of what is coming."

We had walked out of town. Now we were on an asphalt country road. There were woods on both sides of the road, no houses. It was a beautiful area. I didn't know where we were going. As usual, no one told me anything.

Lieutenant Laurie talked to me as if I were an old friend. He commented on a hawk flying low to get a better look at us. He commented on the kinds of trees in the woods. It was sort of like a nature walk for him.

His speech had the musical cadence of the South. He was calm, soft-spoken, exquisitely courteous. I suddenly realized: this is a Southern gentleman, a real one, the first one I had ever met. I liked him immensely. This was very important to me, because if you're going to die, you want to die with someone you like. You don't want to die with someone you don't like.

Captain O'Neill radioed us. We stopped. Lieutenant Laurie took the receiver and stood alongside me. He spoke into the receiver without any stress in his voice whatsoever. I couldn't get over his calmness. I heard one word that caused my heart to skip a beat. It was *boats*.

After Lieutenant Laurie handed me back the receiver, he said matter-of-factly to me, "We're going to cross the river."

Oh, Jesus. I was as good as dead. I remembered the carnage of the Sauer River crossing, the boats riddled with bullets. And I was with a guy who was going to get in the lead boat and I was going to be in there with him. With this guy I had no chance. If Captain O'Neill had been here and I was his radio operator, I would have had a better chance. Captain O'Neill did not lead his men. If there was a line of soldiers walking single file toward the front, the last guy in line would be Captain O'Neill. He marched behind everybody. That was how he had lasted so long. But I was with a guy who led his troops. I had no chance.

This was a suicide mission. That's why they had chosen a totally green officer to lead it. He was fresh meat, expendable. Captain O'Neill was saving his more experienced officers. Right now these officers were probably back in the kitchen, sitting around and drinking coffee. And that was why Captain O'Neill hadn't sent his own radio operator. He was saving him. I was expendable, too. He didn't give a shit about me.

This was going to be my last day on earth. I thought of my mother. She was going to take this hard. There wasn't a thing I could do about it, no place to hide, no one to appeal to. I looked lingeringly at the blue sky, at the trees in the woods. I wouldn't be seeing them anymore. Behind me there was no talking whatsoever. Each man was isolated, sunk in his own thoughts. They knew.

There was one man between me and the whole goddamn German Army. How the hell had this happened? How had I gotten here?

One thing I knew for sure. This was no misunderstanding between Captain O'Neill and Lieutenant Spinner. I thought back to Lieutenant Spinner at the trailer. When he told me to take the radio to Captain O'Neill, he had looked away. He hadn't been able to look me in the eye. He had been ashamed of what he was doing. I hadn't thought about it at the time, his not being able to look at me, but now I saw it clearly. He had deliberately lied to me. He knew what he was sending me into. He had set me up.

It was unprecedented to send battalion staff personnel to do a rifle company's work. It just wasn't done. We had our sphere, they had theirs, and the two were not interchangeable. If three or four officers from a rifle company were killed or badly wounded, that company had to do the best they could without them. No matter how dire the situation, battalion staff officers were never sent forward to take the place, not even temporarily, of the fallen officers. Later, when the rifle company was relieved, it would receive new replacement officers.

And the same thing applied to enlisted men at the battalion staff level. They were never sent to take over rifle company duties. But it was done in this case. Why? I racked my brains, trying to figure it out, but I couldn't.

Lieutenant Spinner had selected me for this. Why? What did he have against me? What had I done to deserve this? I had never said or done anything against him.

Then it hit me. It was as plain as the nose on my face. Lieutenant Spinner hated me because I had seen him cry that night in the OP, sobbing, blubbering helplessly, out of control. When I first met him, he had been grumpy, distant, and unfriendly, as he was with everybody. But after that night I would catch him staring at me with an icy coldness. I did not see the connection then but I did now.

He must have thought I had told some of the guys about the crying, but I hadn't. It was nobody's business but his. And I was smart enough to know that if I had told anybody, it would inevitably get back to him, and he would cut my throat for it.

It was my bad luck to have been at the OP that night, the only enlisted man present. It was going to cost me my life. I was going to die because I had seen him cry. It was as simple as that.

I felt a strong sense of betrayal. He was my commanding officer. He was supposed to protect me, to look out for me. Instead he had offered me up.

I felt a sudden overwhelming surge of hatred for him. He was trying to get me killed. I was filled with blind rage.

And then, paranoia, always close to the surface with me, kicked in. Did everybody know he was going to do this to me? Were they all in on it? Was that why my so-called friends hadn't been around the house this morning? They didn't want to witness it. And was that why Sergeant Drummond had disappeared? He didn't have the heart to do this to me and so had absented himself and forced Spinner to do his own dirty work.

Then I got a terrible thought. Even if I lived through this, maybe this wasn't a one-shot deal. Maybe I was being eased into a permanent assignment with George Company.

An 88 came whistling out of the blue sky down upon us. We all hit the deck. Several more came and we stayed prone. Now Lieutenant Laurie was finding out what war was all about, I thought to myself. How would he take it? When we got to our feet, I peered into his face. A close call with an 88 has a way of making the face disheveled. I studied his eyes for signs of panic or fear. There were none. He was still perfectly calm. He gave me a sheepish smile.

The Germans were telling us they knew we were coming. Great. They would be on the other side of the river, dug in, waiting for us with their rifles, automatic weapons, and machine guns. It would be another blood bath like the Sauer River crossing, where the resistance was fanatical.

How did they know we were coming? I couldn't figure it out. How could they possibly see us? The trees were tall on both sides of the road. And the road meandered this way and that. There was no way they could stand at the end of the road and get a clear view of us. Yet they knew we were here.

We continued down the road but we didn't get far. They started shelling us in earnest. We'd take a few steps, throw ourselves down, get up, take a few more steps, throw ourselves down again. But they weren't hitting us. Close but no cigar.

Progress was slow and I think Lieutenant Laurie was worried that sooner or later somebody was going to be hit and, most likely, more than one guy, so he took us off the road. We followed him, still single file, into the woods on our right.

But the woods were not level. We were on a slope that was like a hillside. It was awkward walking, one leg was up and one leg was down. Walking was hard work. We started sweating and panting. Sometimes you had to grab a bush to maintain your balance.

Finally the slope became too precipitous for us to continue. Lieutenant Laurie took us back up to the road. The shelling had stopped. We walked along. We came to the boats. They were hidden in the bushes on the left-hand side of the road. They had been left there for us by the engineers. Lieutenant Laurie ignored the boats. But we had to be close to the river.

Lieutenant Laurie slowed down. He took us back into the woods. The woods had leveled out quite a bit. We went forward slowly. We crouched down low. Then we came to the edge of the woods. Lieutenant Laurie, myself, and three or four other guys were in a line at the edge, peeking out. We were on our knees. Lieutenant Laurie had his binoculars out.

I looked out. There was a river. It looked deep enough to drown in but, unlike the Sauer, it was relatively narrow. There was a bridge across it. The Germans had not blown it up. There was a town directly across the river. Cross the bridge and you were in the town. I looked at the houses. I couldn't see any signs of life. God, how I wished for 20-20 vision at that moment.

Lieutenant Laurie slowly panned the whole town, going from building to building. Then he did it again.

"I see a girl with a cow," he said, and the way he said it, it sounded like good news.

He radioed back to Captain O'Neill and told him where we were. Then he panned the town again.

Very deliberately we proceeded out of the woods and toward the bridge, Lieutenant Laurie in the lead, me behind him. Everybody had their weapon ready. I had my carbine ready. Everybody was superalert, looking every which way.

We got on the bridge. My heart was pounding. Every step was an adventure. I was expecting some shit at any moment.

Nothing.

We got off the bridge and started down the street, still superalert.

People started coming out of their houses. They stood in little groups, staring at us.

We walked the length of the town. It was a small town. Nothing happened.

Lieutenant Laurie radioed Captain O'Neill and gave him the good news. The town was cleared.

It was a miracle. Not a single shot had been fired. My luck had held out once more. I had my life back. I was elated. I wanted to pound Lieutenant Laurie on the back and scream with happiness but, of course, I did nothing of the sort.

Soon the battalion vehicles started coming across the bridge. They parked all over the place. We had started in the morning but by now it was late afternoon. We would sleep in this town tonight.

I was surrounded by my radio crew. They hovered over me. They were very solicitous. I could see by their faces that they had been very worried about me. They asked me many questions and hung on my every word. They took my radio and put it in the trailer for me, an unheard-of courtesy. I think they felt I had returned from the land of the dead and it might well have turned out that way. Pure chance had determined the outcome.

Jelich told me later the radio crew had been shocked when they found out what had happened. They went to Sergeant Drummond in a state of near-mutiny. An angry Sergeant Drummond then confronted Lieutenant Spinner and secured from him an assurance that this would never happen again.

I knew that there was an element of self-interest in all this. If the radio operators hadn't protested, the next time it could be one of them who was sent to a rifle company. And Sergeant Drummond was concerned because if I had been killed or wounded, then he would have been faced with the headache of trying to find an experienced radio operator to replace me. And in the ensuing shortage, he might have been forced to lug a radio around himself.

I thought of Lieutenant Laurie and the infantrymen I had been with this day. The poor bastards. I was out of it now, but for them it was just another day. Tomorrow they might not be so lucky. Tomorrow the Germans might stand and fight.

I hadn't liked Spinner before, but now I felt such repugnance, it was all I could do to look at him. He had tried to get me killed. That's hard to forgive.

Not too long after this, he was wounded. He got a chunk of shrapnel in the ass. It wasn't a terribly serious wound but it was bad enough that he wouldn't be back.

"Good," I said to myself when I heard the news. "Good riddance. I hope I never see your ugly face again in this life, you son of a bitch."

10

Whitewash

NORMALLY THE BATTALION CP would be set up on the first floor of a two-story house. That way you had a little bit of protection overhead. But this particular two-story house had had its roof and the ceiling of the second story blown off by a shell before we got there, so we retreated below the first floor. We set up the CP in a small room in the cellar. The room had no windows so we had to use the white-gas lamps even during daylight.

The Germans started shelling the town in earnest. The 88s were landing all around us. We looked at each other with apprehension.

Then, like we were one man, we dove for the floor. One was coming in on us. It was a direct hit smack into our house. There was a tremendous, deafening explosion. It sounded like it was a foot from my head. I thought for sure the shell had come through the rough floorboards above to blow us all up. There was a violent shaking of the house like in an earthquake. But our ceiling held.

The room was so small we were practically lying on top of one another. Spumoni's head was inches from my head. Spumoni was clutching his beads and mumbling prayers. "For chrissakes, Spumoni," I wanted to say, "what good do you think you're doing? The guy who shot that shell is clutching his beads and praying that the shell hits us. You're both praying to the same God." And yet, why did I write my mother, "Pray for me"?

We just lay there. Nobody was in a hurry to get up. There was always the chance of another one coming in on us. Besides, when you have experienced a blast that almost takes you into the sweet hereafter, the energy is drained out of you. You feel lethargic, weak, almost comatose.

The farmer who owned the house had covered his cellar walls and ceiling with a thick coat of whitewash. The explosion had knocked loose a million particles of the whitewash and sent them into the air. It was like we were in a snowstorm. You couldn't see across the room. Then as the snow gradually settled, I saw a shadowy figure standing by the table. He was covered from head to foot with the snow. It was Colonel Rudd. The crazy son of a bitch hadn't hit the deck like the rest of us. This was a peculiarity of his that I was to observe again later on. He felt it was beneath his dignity to acknowledge the 88s by throwing himself down in frantic haste and pressing against the floor fearfully. He ignored incoming shells. (When he was wounded by an 88, the first words out of my mouth were, "Was he standing when he was hit?" My informant, Jelich, didn't know.)

We started getting up.

We laughed when we saw what we looked like, covered over. We began slapping our clothes to get rid of the snow. Rudd ignored his.

"For a big man, you move pretty fast," an officer said jokingly to a rotund battalion aid man who had come to the CP to deliver a message. The fellow had shown amazing reflexes and agility by beating us all to the floor.

The Air Corps pilot, who had been in close proximity to my legs on the floor, said to me, "I thought we had it rough but it's nothing compared to this. I don't know how you guys stand it."

The pilot was here under a special program. The Army had sent him out to us to experience the everyday life of another branch of the service. The goal was to bring about better understanding between branches.

The pilot was good-looking as all hell. He had that boyish charm. He could have been on a recruiting poster for the Air Corps. He was friendly, talkative, effervescent. He made quite a contrast to our officers, who tended to be a pretty glum lot.

The officers did not welcome him. They seemed to resent him. They acted like he wasn't there, which I thought was a pretty shitty way to treat him. So out of loneliness, he started talking to me. I got the impression from him that the division between officers and enlisted men in the Air Corps was much less rigid than it was in the infantry. He was very much at ease with me. I could tell the officers didn't like him talking to me. It was a "you're-spoiling-the-servants" kind of thing.

He was supposed to stay with us one week, but after four days, he had had enough. He left suddenly. I didn't blame him. I would have left with him if I could have.

The day after the shell hit the house we had another visitor, an inadvertent one. Things had quieted down and I was standing outside the CP, about to go in, when a jeep drove into the yard. The man on the passenger side jumped out and walked briskly toward me. He had a terrific-looking coat, with fur around the collar. I felt warm just looking at it. He was a short, older man. I was startled to see a star on his helmet. A brigadier general. I had never been this close to a general before. Even though we didn't salute officers at the front, this was different. He was a general. I came to attention and gave him a snappy salute. His salute in return was halfhearted, more like a wave.

"Is this Regimental Headquarters?" he asked.

"No, sir," I said. "This is the second battalion CP."

His driver was a couple of steps behind him. The general turned and fixed the driver with a look that could have fried eggs.

"I must have taken a wrong turn coming out of Diekirch," the driver stammered.

"Well, let's go!" the general barked. "I've got things to do!"

They jumped back in the jeep and the driver put a heavy foot down on the accelerator. They zoomed away.

Yes, a lot of people had things to do somewhere else when they were at the front.

11

Jelich and the Roll

WHEN WE PULLED INTO TOWN, Sergeant Drummond was waiting for us. He directed us to a house. It looked like we would be here for two or three days. We took our bedding off the trailer and trooped into the house. It was a nice house, nothing pretentious about it, but well built, sturdy, and very neat and clean.

It wasn't time for chow yet so we spent a few minutes looking around the big living room where later we would spread our blankets and sleep.

There was a porcelain pipe displayed on the wall. I couldn't get over it—it was so beautiful. There were lovely flowers painted on the foot-long stem, red roses and other flowers of similar brilliance. I wondered: Had this pipe ever been smoked or was it an art object, a decoration? Maybe the grandfather had smoked it and it was a family heirloom.

There were no pictures of Hitler on the wall but there was a framed head shot of Kaiser Wilhelm when he was in his prime, vigorous, proud, with that big handlebar mustache. He looked thick-headed and I guess he was. It's not good for a country to be ruled by a dummy.

Hillbilly was rummaging around in a china closet. It was exactly like the one we had at home, except that this one was quite a bit bigger. It was not freestanding but was built into the wall. It had two glass doors that met in the middle. My mother kept all her wedding china in hers, plates of all sizes, cups, saucers, etc. She never used any of them, not even on special occasions. "Why don't you use them?" I asked her. "If I used them, they'd all be broken by now," she said. "I wouldn't have any left."

Hillbilly yelled out, "Hey, look what I found!"

He held a teapot in his left hand. From it he plucked a fat roll of bills. He held the roll up for all to see.

"I got me *beaucoup* marks!" He pronounced it *boo-coo.*

Nobody commented on his find.

Spumoni stood by the wall in front of a framed photograph, staring at it.

"Charley, come over here," he said.

I went over to him.

"What does that say?" he said, pointing to some handwriting on the lower left-hand corner of the photograph.

It was a group picture of three boys, taken in a studio. They were standing side by side, looking straight ahead, directly at the camera. They were about eight years old. They were clean and scrubbed, in their Sunday best.

The writing said *Die Erste Heilige Kommunion.*

"The first Holy Communion," I said.

Spumoni was aghast.

"I didn't know the Germans were Catholic," he said.

"Well, they are in this part of Germany. I think that when you go north or east, then they're Protestant, Lutheran."

"How could they be Catholic?"

"Well, they are," I said tartly.

"How could they be Catholic and start the war?"

"I don't know," I said. "You'll have to ask them."

There was a soft knock on the door. Somebody peeked out the window.

The cry went out. "There's a Kraut at the door! Charley, go see what he wants!"

I went over and opened the door. It was a grizzled old man who looked to be in his fifties. He was wearing those high black boots all the German farmers seemed to wear. He stood there, cap in hand, stammering, very fearful. He looked like he might pass out. He lived in this house. He had forgotten something. He asked for permission to come in and get it. His eyes beseeched me.

I let him in.

Hillbilly objected.

"What the hell's he doing in here? There's not supposed to be any Krauts in here!"

"He forgot something," I said. "I'll keep my eye on him. I'll be responsible for him."

Still holding his cap in his hand, he bowed his way to everybody all the way across the room, straight to the china closet. He opened it and started poking around in it. He was very, very nervous and kept glancing over his shoulder at us. He found the teapot and opened it and turned around and gave us a terrible look of dismay. He started mumbling to himself and continued looking.

I guess Jelich was affected by his distress.

"Why don't you give him back his money, Hillbilly?" Jelich suggested.

"Screw him! What's he ever done for me?"

"It's not much to you but it's probably all the poor old guy has."

"Tough shit. I didn't ask to be sent over here."

"You can't use it anyway. There's nothing to spend it on."

"What's wrong with you? It seems like you're getting mighty considerate of these Krauts," Hillbilly said, insinuatingly.

Jelich just shook his head in disgust.

(The next day Hillbilly asked me privately, "Is Jelich German?" "No," I said. "He's Croatian." Hillbilly blinked. I knew he didn't have the foggiest notion where Croatia was.)

The man left then and Jelich and I went to chow soon after.

"I can't get mad at these people, Charley," Jelich said. "You know why? Because when I see that old guy, I see my own father. My father looks just like him. And he reminds me of my father in little ways. He's from the old country, you know. That's why I can't push these people around. It would be like pushing my own father around. And if my father was ever in a situation like this, I would want him treated right."

The next morning everybody took off except Jelich and me. There was a knock on the door. It was the farmer again. He asked for permission to look some more.

I let him in.

He went straight to the china closet and started moving stuff around. But his heart wasn't in it. He knew he wasn't going to find anything. I had a feeling his wife made him come back and look some more. Soon he quit and closed the glass doors.

He turned and looked at us and pointed at himself, jabbing himself several times in the chest with his thumb.

"*In dem Wald arbeiten*," he said.

"He works in the woods," I translated for Jelich.

"*Ja*," he said, nodding vigorously, as if I had translated him correctly.

He went over to the wall and beckoned to me. I went over. He was standing in front of the *Die Erste Heilige Kommunion* picture. He put his finger on the boy in the middle.

"*Mein Sohn*," he said.

The boy was too serious, like he could see into the future.

"*Er ist sehr schön*," I said.

I knew that *schön* meant beautiful and wasn't the right word to use for a boy, but I didn't know the word for good-looking. Not that he was all that good-looking but I felt it was a nice thing to say.

"*Ja*," he said, nodding, as if agreeing with me. "*Er war ein guter Junge. Immer ein guter Junge.*"

"He was a good boy. Always a good boy," I told Jelich.

Tears rolled down the man's cheeks. He turned away from us so we wouldn't see them.

"*Tot in Russland.*"

"Dead in Russia," I said.

"*Meine Frau*, every night, she goes to bed," he said in German and he twisted his head down and put two hands under it, pantomiming her lying on the pillow. "All night long, she cries and cries." He repeatedly ran the fingers of both hands down his cheeks, pantomiming the copious flow of tears. "She can't sleep anymore. That was six months ago and she still cries all night long. You see, he was our only child," he said in explanation.

I thought of my mother. I felt a deep sadness for this man and his wife. I knew that their anguish would be with them for as long as they lived. Now hold on a minute here, I thought. Should I be feeling sorrow at the death of a German soldier who, if he had been on the Western front, would have been trying to kill me? This was weird. What should I be feeling?

The man left then, and Jelich said, "I think that ninety per cent of the world is made up of quiet guys like him. They don't know what's going on. They just want to work and mind their own business and live a quiet life. But the other ten per cent, they're the ones who start the wars and get the quiet guys to kill each other."

That was as good an explanation as any, I thought. The ten per cent were the clever people. And when the deluge came, sweeping everything before it, the clever people always managed to come out of it all right. They knew how to take care of themselves.

12

Footsteps

THE BATTALION WAS on the move again. The snow on the ground had lost its luster and turned gray, but fresh snow started falling. Soon the ground was again covered with a pristine whiteness. We drove through it to the next town where we relieved another battalion from our regiment. We set up the battalion CP.

"There's nobody between us and the Krauts," Colonel Rudd announced. "I want every house to post a guard tonight."

We had never posted a guard at any house before. We had always had a rifle company between us and the enemy. This time it was different. The battalion was spread so thin on the line that there was no rifle company in front of us.

I had stood a lot of guard duty back in the States but this would be the first time overseas. The communications guys were all at one house. Sergeant Drummond assigned the reliefs. Hillbilly would be on from midnight to two. I would be on from two to four. At two Hillbilly came upstairs and woke me. I was sleeping with my overcoat on so all I had to do was put on my boots and grab my helmet. I went downstairs. Hillbilly was waiting for me in front of the house. He went up to bed and I took over.

It was a cold, crisp, dark night. The snow had stopped coming down.

Hillbilly had been standing in front of the doorway. That's not such a good idea, I thought. You're out in the open. You can be seen. It's better to be hidden.

I went and stood inside the doorway and just stuck my head out. I was peeking around the corner, toward the left. To the left was the front. That was the direction the Germans would come from. To the right were other houses and other guards. Unfortunately, we were the last house on the street. The Germans would come to us first. Our house was by itself, set off from the other houses. I did not like this isolation.

The night was still, absolutely quiet. I began to relax. Suddenly— *what was that?* I thought I heard a sound. Instantly I became rigid, staring into the dark and listening with every atom in my body.

I heard it clearly. The crunching of snow. Unmistakable. A footstep. *Oh, my God!* Somebody was out there, out there in the street in front of the house and to the left.

I didn't want to be a standing target. I immediately got down on my stomach and swung around to face the left. I took the safety off the carbine and got in position to fire. I had a round in the chamber.

It was quiet again.

Then another footstep. Just one stealthy footstep. I realized he had stopped and was *listening for me just as I was listening for him.*

I knew one thing. I absolutely was not going to challenge him with the password and give away my location. The second I saw him, I was going to fire. A week earlier, a sergeant in the anti-tank platoon had been standing behind a tree sometime after midnight. He saw a lone figure coming up the road. The sergeant assumed it was an American. He stepped out from behind the tree and gave the password, expecting to hear the countersign. But it was a German and he whipped out a burp gun, shot the sergeant dead, and then disappeared back down the road.

Footsteps. *Oh, Jesus.* That sounded like more than one man. Was it a patrol? Would they have burp guns and grenades? What chance would I have against a patrol? Then quiet again.

I cursed the Army. I had one clip in the carbine and another one in my cartridge belt. Why were they so stingy with their ammunition? I didn't want to husband bullets. I wanted to fire and keep firing.

I hoped the firing would waken the fellows. If it didn't, they could be shot as they lay sleeping.

I cursed my fate. Circumstances had placed me in a position I dreaded most of all—having my life depend on my ability to see. Especially at night when my sight was even worse than it was in the daylight.

Footsteps again—real close.

I stared into the darkness. I willed my eyes to see. My eyes bugged out of my head with the effort. My finger was taut on the trigger.

Then out of the darkness he stepped into my field of vision. It was a pig, a big one. He had his snout close to the ground, sniffing around. He was not snorting or making any kind of pig noises. He meandered past our house and continued down the street.

I just lay there. I felt too weak, too drained to get up. I was expecting burp guns and grenades. Instead I got a pig. I had lucked out one more time. It had been a terrifying several minutes. An 88 comes at you so fast you barely have time to draw a breath. This was different. I had time to think. Is it possible to be so scared your pounding heart bursts through your chest?

The next morning I didn't tell anybody what had happened. I didn't want to be the butt of jokes from now until the end of the war.

About ten in the morning, Sergeant Drummond came around.

"Spumoni, Hillbilly, and Charley," he said, "you three guys go to the CP. There's a 2 1/2 ton truck with a driver just outside the CP. He's going to take you to Third Army Headquarters in Luxembourg. You're going to pick up a load of coal. This is a real good sign. They wouldn't be sending us back for coal if we weren't going to sit here for a while."

We showed up at the truck. The driver was waiting for us. Hillbilly sat up front in the cab with him. Spumoni and I climbed into the back. We sat by the tailgate on opposite ends of the benches and looked at the countryside as we drove through it.

"You know what I don't understand?" Spumoni said. "Why did the Germans attack the French? Look at these farms. You don't see farms like this in France. The Germans have better land than the French. They have better houses. They have better barns. They have everything better. The French farmers are poor compared to the German ones. So you'd think it would be the French attacking the Germans. Instead it's the other way around. If everything in your country is better than the other guy's country, why would you attack him? It doesn't make sense."

We drove many miles and in the early afternoon arrived at the city of Luxembourg. We entered along a broad boulevard lined with trees. Every tree had sticks of dynamite wrapped around its trunk and wired for detonation. I surmised this was because of the surprise attack of the Germans in mid-December. The Allies had been afraid the Germans were on their way to Luxembourg and the dynamite was a defensive measure. If the trees were blown up, they would fall across the road and so impede German motorized traffic. Or so I conjectured.

There were no civilians on the sidewalks, just American military personnel. There was a ton of officers, lots in the middle ranks, captains, majors, highlighted by an occasional general. There were lots of sergeants. I saw very few privates. Some war correspondents came walking down the street, six abreast. They were in their helmets and trench coats. Three of them were smoking pipes. That's kind of a leisurely type of smoking. I never saw a pipe at the front.

There was an orgy of saluting going on. Everywhere you looked, somebody was snappily applying a rigid hand to his forehead. All the officers were walking briskly. That's in the officer's handbook. "You must walk briskly at all times. Act like you're going someplace important."

But I noticed everybody basically had a carefree expression. These were people without any real worries. In life there are the favored and the unfavored, those who live well and those who get it up the ass, the lords and the peasants. At college I had been a lord. In this war I was a peasant. And all these people here in the city of Luxembourg, they were the favored. They could cancel their life insurance without risk. But Spumoni and Hillbilly and I were just visitors. We would pick up our load of coal and then drive away from this city of the living, back toward the land of death. And these people here wouldn't lose any sleep over it. That was life.

The driver took us to a supply yard that had huge piles of coal. He backed the truck up to one pile. There were shovels sticking in the piles. The three of us each grabbed a shovel and started shoveling the coal up into the truck. The truck driver took off. He wasn't about to shovel coal. Hillbilly climbed into the truck to push the coal further back on the bed.

Then I got an idea.

"Guys," I said. "I'm going to give you a choice. I can stay here and shovel coal with you. Or I can go out and try to get us something to eat. It's up to you. Which do you want me to do?"

"Go out and try to get us something to eat!" Hillbilly said with feeling.

I looked at Spumoni.

"Yeah," Spumoni said, nodding approval.

"Look," I said. "I'm not guaranteeing you anything. I could come back empty-handed."

"Just do your best," Spumoni said.

If I came back empty-handed, it would look like I was gold-bricking just to get out of some work, but that was the chance I was taking.

I left the yard and walked down a couple of streets. I found a kitchen and walked in. It was on the street level of a building. There was only one cook on duty, a short Italian guy with a robust mustache. He was alone in there. His eyes opened wide when he saw me.

I walked up to him.

"Hi," I said.

"Hi," he said. "You from the front?"

"Yeah," I said, nodding.

I was dirty and unshaven. It was obvious I was from the front. I didn't feel dirty at the front. Everybody was dirty there. But here everybody was clean. I stood out like a sore thumb.

"How are things up there?"

I laughed a little.

"Pretty bad, actually."

I could see the wonder and awe in his eyes. I was counting on his sympathy. Let him assume I was a rifleman. I wasn't going to tell him different.

"I'm up here to get some coal," I said. "I missed lunch. Any chance you could give me something to eat?"

"Sure," he said. "Sit down."

He brought me some kind of meat loaf and mashed potatoes. It wasn't hot but I didn't mind that. I polished it off in good time.

"I'm up here with two buddies," I said. "They didn't get any lunch either. Any chance you could give me something to take back to them?"

He looked around. He was thinking. Then he went behind the counter and reached up and pulled down a whole salami that was hanging from a hook and gave it to me. It must have been eight inches long.

"Gee, thanks," I said. "You've been really great. I appreciate it."

He was the nicest cook I had ever come across.

"It's the least I could do for what you guys are doing," he said.

We shook hands.

"Good luck," he said.

"Thanks," I said. "You, too."

I found my way back to the guys. It was perfect timing. They had just finished loading the truck.

I showed them the salami.

They were ecstatic.

"How did you get it?" they asked, their eyes wide with admiration.

I didn't tell them I had already had my own private lunch.

The driver showed up and we took off. This time Hillbilly sat in the back with me and Spumoni. Fortunately, Spumoni had a jack-knife. We turned the salami over to him. As we drove along, he would cut a slice off and hand it to each of us in turn. His hands were black with coal dust. It didn't bother me a bit. When you're hungry, the niceties go out the window damned fast.

"Boy, this is good!" Hillbilly said.

"Yeah, it sure is," Spumoni said. "This is the first salami I've had since I left home."

The truth was: It was delicious. More than delicious.

"I don't know how you do it, Charley," Spumoni said. "You always go out and come back with something."

I laughed.

It was just luck this time. If I had come back empty-handed, he wouldn't have been so happy.

We polished off the whole salami long before we got back. They were happy. I was happy. All in all, a good day.

13

The Luger

COLONEL RUDD WANTED TO GO forward to confer with Captain O'Neill of George Company but he didn't want to risk his jeep because there was shell fire up ahead so he left the vehicle parked alongside the road with me and Jelich in it and he walked the rest of the way to George Company's CP.

Jelich and I relaxed in the jeep. I was in the back seat with my radio and Jelich was behind the wheel. There was an open field on my right and a house set back from the road on my left. The house was back and up higher than the road so the walk leading to the house had rising wooden steps. Instead of a fence the house had a five-foot-high stone wall running a few feet from the road.

Suddenly I caught a movement out of the corner of my left eye. I turned my head and looked at the house. Holy shit! Two German soldiers were coming down the walk with their hands on their heads. I jumped out of the jeep with my carbine at the ready. Jelich had reacted to my hasty move and he too now got out of the jeep. Jelich carried a pistol, an Army .45, on his hip, which he now took out of the holster.

I was upset. This area was supposed to have been cleared. How had these two guys been overlooked? Had they wanted to, they could have shot Jelich and me easily from the house as we sat there, idly talking, perfect targets.

We waited for the Germans to get to us. One was an enlisted man. The other was an officer. The officer kept his eyes on us but he was chatting at the enlisted man in a one-sided conversation. He was smiling and even broke into a laugh. I was dumbfounded. He wasn't acting the way I imagined a soldier who was surrendering would act, with fear and trepidation. This guy was acting like he didn't have a care in the world. I didn't understand German well enough to know what he was saying to the enlisted man. The enlisted man had more sense. He looked worried.

Neither man carried a weapon and they both were bareheaded. I motioned where I wanted them to stand. They were on the grassy side of the road, a few feet in front of the stone wall. They stood facing us. If the officer had kept talking, I would have told him to *"Nicht sprechen,"* but he had shut up.

I looked him over. This was no lowly second lieutenant. From his bearing and the prominent, twisted silver braid on his shoulders, I guessed that he was an officer of the middle rank, a major or a colonel. He was quite handsome. He had wavy silvery hair. It was prematurely silvery. He looked to be in his forties. He was clean-shaven. His uniform was immaculate. He was of medium height, trim-figured.

"What are we going to do with them?" I asked Jelich. "We can't send them back on their own and when Rudd gets here, he's not going to want to fuck around with two prisoners."

Jelich thought it over.

"Why don't you call Tidwell on your radio? He's in charge of prisoners. Ask him what to do."

"That's a good idea," I said.

I went across the road to the jeep, keeping an eye on the prisoners all the while, and radioed Tidwell. He was at the battalion CP back in town.

I explained the situation to him. He didn't seem too interested. Then I said, "One of them's an officer."

"I'll be right there!" he said.

In a few minutes Tidwell drove up at a good clip. He was alone in a jeep.

He parked behind our jeep. He jumped out and rushed over to us. He was all excited.

"Did he have a Luger? Did he have a Luger?" he was asking even before he got to us.

"They didn't have any weapons," I said.

"Damn! I want to get my hands on a Luger in the worst way! Damn it!"

What nerve Tidwell had, I was thinking. He was automatically assuming the Luger was his, if there had been a Luger. The prisoners had surrendered to Jelich and me, not him. The Luger, if there had been a Luger, rightly belonged to Jelich and me. It was finders-keepers. That's what happened when a rifleman chanced upon a German officer with a Luger. He took it off him and kept it. That's why Tidwell never was able to get a Luger from the prisoners he was in charge of. By the time they got to him, they had been de-Lugered by the riflemen. I didn't want a goddamn Luger. I had no use for a Luger. I wanted to carry around books in civilian life, not Lugers. But his assumption that the Luger, if there had been one, belonged to him really irritated me.

The German officer was smiling at Tidwell, like he was enjoying the joke.

I guess that was the last straw for Tidwell.

"What the hell are you laughing at?" Tidwell cried angrily. "You goddamn *Schweinhund!*"

He went over to the officer and spun him around roughly. Then he gave him a mighty shove toward the wall. "You, too!" he snarled at the enlisted man, who speedily complied.

Now the two Germans were up against the wall with their backs to us.

The German officer was no longer smiling. After an initial look of surprise, his face showed great alarm. He kept glancing over his shoulder at Tidwell. *"Nicht schiessen!"* he said. *"Nicht schiessen!"* He thought Tidwell was going to shoot him.

But Tidwell wasn't going to shoot him. He was just pissed off. After a while, he calmed down. He sat the two prisoners on the hood of his jeep and drove slowly back to town.

Jelich and I returned to our jeep.

"All Tidwell cares about is the number of prisoners taken," Jelich said. "That's all he's good for, counting prisoners. That and looting. He's the biggest looter in the battalion. He spends all his time looking for stuff to send back home. Every time we get relieved, he sends a package home."

I knew about that. The other officers kidded him about it. "Did you get much loot in such-and-such a town?" they'd say. Tidwell always corrected them. "Souvenirs," he'd say. "Souvenirs."

"Did you hear what happened between Tidwell and Captain O'Neill the other day?" Jelich asked.

"No, I didn't," I said.

"George Company had had a rough day and they were walking back into town. Easy Company took over for them. And Tidwell was waiting on the road for Captain O'Neill to come by. When Captain O'Neill came up to him, Tidwell says, 'Well, how many did we bag today, Neely?'

"And Captain O'Neill says, 'None.'

"Tidwell looks all surprised. 'None?' he says, like he couldn't believe it.

"And Tidwell's tone of voice pisses Captain O'Neill off. He took it as criticism, you know. 'Yes, none!' he says. He grabs a rifle off the nearest dogface and he offers it to Tidwell. 'Here, you want a couple? Go get them!'

"'Gee, we're getting mighty touchy, aren't we?' Tidwell says.

"All the guys in George Company got a big laugh out of it."

Poor Lieutenant Tidwell. I actually liked the guy. He was just trying to get through this thing, like everybody else. I think the looting was just a distraction for him. Something to keep his mind occupied and make him feel the war was not a total waste of his time.

14

A Dirty Trick

FOX COMPANY TOOK THE TOWN and then set up a defensive line outside it. This was one lucky town. The German soldiers had pulled out without firing a shot so there was no shelling of the town. It was the luck of the draw. The Germans might make a determined stand at the next town and it would be pulverized by our artillery. But here the houses were untouched.

Strangely enough, the townspeople had fled with their troops, or maybe before the troops. They probably had been expecting a bombardment, which didn't happen. The town was empty. Good, we wouldn't have to bother with kicking people out of their homes.

We rolled into town. I was in the back of Jelich's jeep. Groton was in the front seat with him and Hillbilly was in the back seat with me. We were pulling the radio trailer.

Sergeant Drummond was out in the street, waiting for us. We drove up to him.

"Easy and George will be here in fifteen minutes, so move fast," Sergeant Drummond said. "Right now, you guys get your pick of the houses. Let's pick out a good one."

We looked around.

There was one house that clearly stood out from its neighbors. It was very well kept up and radiated prosperity. It had dramatic windows. But it was the front door that told you everything. It was a massive door, looked twelve inches thick, with beautiful carvings on its face.

"Bring in your bedding and spread it around, so everybody will know we claim it," Sergeant Drummond said.

We collected our bedding from the trailer and trooped into the house. Hillbilly had gone on inside because his bedding was not in our trailer.

"The dirty lousy fuckin' Krauts!" It was a ringing cry of disbelief from Hillbilly.

Hillbilly was standing in what I supposed was the dining room. There on the floor in the middle of the room was a pile of feces, a welcoming gift from the German soldiers I presumed.

We all stood around and looked at it.

"This is really disgusting," Sergeant Drummond said with a grimace.

"What a dirty trick!" Hillbilly said. "Those bastards!"

Hillbilly didn't get this worked up from an 88 shelling. You expected that. But this was a breach of the rules of civilized warfare.

"I wonder if one man did this," Groton said.

"It would take a horse to shit this much," Jelich said.

"I don't mean in one day but in two or three days," Groton explained.

"I'd say there were at least two different men," Jelich said. "There's brown shit on the bottom and yellow shit on top."

"Well, we've got to clean it up," Sergeant Drummond said. "Hillbilly, flip a coin with Charley. The loser cleans it up."

Jelich pulled out a fifty-cent piece from his pocket.

"Who's going to call it?"

"I'll call it," Hillbilly said.

"Call it in the air," Jelich said.

Jelich flipped.

"Tails!" Hillbilly said.

Jelich caught the coin in his right hand and turned it over on the back of his left hand.

We all leaned close to look.

"Heads," Jelich said. "You lose, Hillbilly."

"Shit!"

"That's right," Jelich said. "And lots of it."

"Let's find another house," Hillbilly said.

"Now be a good sport," Jelich said. "You lost fair and square."

"How am I supposed to clean it?" Hillbilly protested in dismay.

"There's a bunch of shingles in the yard," Sergeant Drummond said. "Take one of them and slide it under the pile. You'll get most of it, maybe all of it. If there's any left, look around in the kitchen. There'll be some rags there, towels, use them. Just wipe it off. Then take the rug by the door and throw it over the spot."

"You're in luck, Hillbilly," Jelich said. "This shit looks hard. They could have had the runs."

"I'd say it's more medium soft," I said.

My escaping this job had made me merry.

"And afterwards, Hillbilly," I said, "you take that shingle down to the cooks and show them what shit on a shingle really looks like. It'll help them with their cooking."

Everybody laughed, except Hillbilly.

I burst into song.

> *Dinner for one, please James,*
> *Madam will not be dining,*
> *Yes you may bring the wine in,*
> *Love plays such funny games.*

Jelich and I left then to explore the house.

There was a staircase going to the second floor. It was like something you saw in a movie. It was wide and curved around and looked like it was made of marble. We went up it.

We went into a bedroom. What a spacious bedroom! We had three bedrooms in my house back home. Put them all together and they would have been smaller in area than this one.

There was a huge bed up against the wall. I never saw a bed this big. And there was a lot of space around it. You didn't bump into things and have to walk sideways like you did in my bedroom back home.

There was a soft, thick rug over the entire floor. We went over to a closet. It was built into the wall. It had sliding doors so you could just reach in and take out what you wanted. But the amazing thing was this closet ran the whole length of the room and was packed with clothes.

To my surprise, when we inspected the clothes, we discovered that they were all women's clothes. This house belong to a woman! As we found out later, there was no evidence in the entire house of a male presence.

There were a few dresses but her clothing was mostly suits. Then we came to a section in the closet of uniforms. She must have had ten uniforms. They had Nazi insignias on them and swastika arm bands.

"She must have been a big shot," Jelich said.

"Yeah," I said. From the size of her clothes, definitely a big shot. She was clearly a pretty beefy, strapping woman. One might even say a mountain of a woman. Judging from the circumference of the upper arms of her sleeves, she could have been a weight lifter.

There was a nightstand at the head of her bed. We went over to it. On it was a book. I picked it up and leafed through the pages. It was a book of photographs by Heinrich Hoffmann. The whole book was on the Polish campaign. Page after page showed pictures of German soldiers grinning at the camera. It was a picnic for them. There were a lot of motorcycles. There were some pictures of smoking ruins of buildings but no pictures of any dead.

By this book was a small red case made of fine leather. It was about the size of a 3-by-5 card. There was an inverted triangle on the front of the case. Inside the triangle was pale gold lettering that read *Nat. Soz. Frauenschaft.* Below that, but still inside the triangle, was a white crucifix on a black background, and on the cross instead of Christ there was a small red swastika at its center. I opened the case. Inside was a pocket with a window. The pocket was for a card of identification, for your picture and particulars. But the pocket was empty. Someone had removed the card from behind the window. I slipped the case into my pocket. I would keep it as a souvenir.

We went into her bathroom. Like her bedroom, it was spacious, not tiny and cramped like mine at home. The floor's surface was very attractive, made up of small shiny green ceramic tile.

We stared at her bathtub. It was not a white bathtub standing by itself. It was a sunken bathtub. It was below the surface of the floor. You stepped down into it. It was round and easily big enough for two or three people, like a miniature swimming pool. It was the first sunken bathtub I had ever seen.

"This is some house," Jelich said.

There was a medicine cabinet built into the wall. Most medicine cabinets are small. This one appeared to be more like a pantry. We opened it. Wow! It was like a drugstore in there. There must have been a hundred bottles of pills lined up on the shelves. I never saw so many pills in my life.

"This is one sick woman," Jelich said. "She must have been the pharmacist's best customer."

Hillbilly was just finishing his cleanup when we came downstairs.

"Good job, Hillbilly," I said. "I give it my Good Housekeeping Seal of Approval."

He gave me a look. Why did I have to say things like that? A comedian's road is a hard one.

A couple of minutes later the front door opened. It was Lieutenant Tidwell. He walked in, looking the place over.

"What are you guys doing in here?" he asked.

"The communications crew is staying here," Jelich said.

"No, you're not," Lieutenant Tidwell said. "Didn't you see the sign out front? This is the battalion CP."

"There was no sign when we came in," Jelich said.

"Well, there is now," Lieutenant Tidwell said with a little laugh. "You better find yourself another place."

Having suffered a reversal of fortune, we now gathered up our belongings, left the mansion, and moved into a more modest dwelling, the better homes all being taken, for now the whole battalion was in town and we had the last selection.

After what he had gone through, Hillbilly was particularly unhappy with the eviction. I wondered if he wasn't tempted to show his displeasure by welcoming the officers with a gift of his own in the middle of the dining room floor and letting them get their own shingle.

We would spend the night in less luxurious surroundings, but it was over with, and after a hot meal, we didn't feel so bad.

That night I stretched out in my blankets and I got to thinking. Something struck me. I suddenly realized that all the guys I had met at the front were nice guys, sweet guys really, almost gentle. I saw it clearly: *There are no tough guys at the front.* I had never seen a fight or a near-fight at the front. I had never heard any threats or harsh words. And that was why I liked the front so much. I liked the front because we didn't have to salute the officers. And I liked the front because we were spared petty, chicken-shit harassing by the noncoms. But the main reason I liked the front was the fellows. I was very much at ease with them. They were the best group of guys I had ever served with. None of them were looking for trouble.

This is odd, I thought. The camps back in the States were loaded with tough guys swaggering about. The Army had fucked up again. If the Army had better psychological testing, they could have identified these tough guys and shipped them to the front. And the mild and peaceable guys who were actually at the front could have been kept in the States where they belonged. If those two groups could have been switched, think of how it could have shortened the war.

That's not to say that some among the mild and peaceable guys were not capable of incredible acts of bravery. Just a few days previously, a lieutenant in Easy Company single-handedly took out an enemy self-propelled gun and captured its crew. He ran up to the SP, put a grenade in the muzzle of its gun, and then trained his carbine on the crew.

Or could I be wrong? Had the Army sent some tough guys to the front and the 88s had pounded all that tough-guy bullshit out of them and turned them into decent human beings? But what would happen after the war and they returned home? In a couple of years, would they forget and become tough guys again?

15

Major Pusey

I
THE COMMANDER

I served under three battalion commanders. The first was Colonel Rudd. He was wounded by an 88 and evacuated. His successor was Major Goode, our former exec officer. Major Goode didn't last long, poor man, before he too was wounded by an 88 and evacuated. I had the good fortune not to be with them when they were wounded. My third and last battalion commander was Major Pusey.

Major Pusey was a big guy, big up and down, and big across. He was bald, except for a little fringe of hair on each side of his head. In manner, he was rude and overbearing. I took an instant dislike to him and he to me.

Major Pusey was sent down to us from Regiment. I guess he was used to a certain rear-echelon level of comfort and service, for he brought with him his own personal flunky, a sharp-eyed guy named Brierly, who doubled as his personal jeep driver. Jelich had driven for battalion commanders but he had other driving assignments also. Brierly drove exclusively for Major Pusey and that was it.

Brierly identified completely with Major Pusey. He was obsequious to the major but haughty with other enlisted men. We learned

early to hold our tongues when he was around, because he would repeat comments to the major.

The first night Major Pusey joined us, he rang for his manservant.
Actually, he opened the door and called to Brierly, who was camped
out in another room.

Brierly brought in a collapsible canvas cot and set it up. Then he
went out and returned with a sleeping bag. He unrolled it on the cot
and carefully smoothed out every wrinkle. He also had brought a pillow. He took the pillow and fluffed it up nicely and set it in place. The
pillow even had a white pillowcase. In the morning Brierly would
come back and reverse the process.

None of the staff officers had a cot. Except for Lieutenant Spinner, none of them had a sleeping bag. They threw their blankets on
the floor, from battalion commanders on down. And none of them
had a pillow, and they certainly didn't have someone to fluff up this
pillow for them.

A commander should not live better than the men in his immediate command. The cot and the pillow were not an amulet, but had
they been, I felt they were bad juju.

II

THE CONQUEROR

We broke through the German lines on the western side of the Rhine.
A combat team or strike force had been assembled. It was to start
south and then swing east. It would meet other elements coming
down from the north, trapping all the German troops inside the
noose.

Strike forces varied in their composition but they always contained two essentials, Sherman tanks in the front followed by half-
tracks loaded with infantrymen. Interspersed among the half-tracks
were two or three jeeps carrying infantry officers. Bringing up the
rear, the very last vehicle in the procession, was a jeep driven by
Brierly, with Major Pusey in the passenger seat, and myself in the
back seat with my radio. Major Pusey was the commander of the
strike force.

The procession started out. There was a healthy interval between vehicles. Bunching up was not a wise thing to do. We were in mountainous country. The farmers grew the crops on the terraced sides of the mountains. There would be one road leading into the town and one road leading out. It was hard to get lost with these towns.

We came to our first town without incident. Somehow the people knew we were coming. White bedsheets, a signal of surrender, hung from every house. A few old women were leaning out of windows. But the rest of the people lined one side of the street to watch us come in. Side by side were women, small children, young girls, young boys, and old men. They watched us intently, silently.

The strike force came to a halt in the town. The vehicles pulled in close behind each other. The people were afraid. This was their first look at the dragon and they didn't know what to expect. This fear wouldn't last long because Americans are not a scary people but at least the fear was here today.

The young people looked at us in awe, like we were powerful, invincible soldiers. But the older people were quaking in their boots, big-eyed, apprehensive. The fear radiated from their eyes like a palpable ray. Being feared is a very heady wine, especially for someone like me who had never been feared by anyone in his whole life. But we had a part to play here. The people obviously expected us to be tough. So everybody tried to look tough. It affected even me. I got out of the jeep to stretch my legs and I walked around with a steely, stern expression on my face.

But what was going on with Major Pusey? He had gotten out of the jeep and started walking to where the other officers were standing around, but he was walking funny. His chest was out, his shoulders were thrown back, and he was walking with his arms thrust out from his sides like an ape or a weight lifter who cannot bring his arms close to his sides because of his overdeveloped muscles. He was gesturing dramatically and declaiming loudly even before he got to the officers. What was he doing? Then it hit me. He was playing up to the audience, the German civilians. The infantrymen had not been allowed off the half-tracks. The tank men had popped up to look around but they didn't get on the ground. The only ones walking around were the lieutenants from the jeeps. And they had gotten into town before Major Pusey. The townspeople were focused on them, watching their every move. What Pusey was doing now was trying to divert the people's attention from the second lieutenants to himself. After all, he was the commander. He wanted the people to know that.

After some time, Major Pusey gave the command and we started for the second town, keeping a good interval again. Pusey was in a foul mood. I knew what was bugging him—his reception in the first town. He didn't like the second lieutenants hogging the limelight. He was coming in on the scene too late. Think of it as a Broadway play. Helen Hayes does not make her first appearance in the third act after everyone else is on stage. No. The curtain goes up and we see a maid dusting the furniture. The butler pops in and they chitchat, gossiping, setting the scene, telling us what to expect. And after two or three minutes of that, suddenly there's Helen Hayes on the landing to the right. She takes one step and stops, lets the applause warm her, and then comes down into the play. Now that's how a star should be treated. Major Pusey was not a playgoer but he had theatrical instincts. He was the commander, the star of this show, and he deserved to be treated as the star. The acknowledgment, the respect, the homage due the star should rightly be his.

Suppose he drove into town first? He would step out of the jeep. He would be the first American soldier the Germans had ever seen, the moment uncontaminated by the presence of some second lieutenants. All eyes would be focused on him. It would be him and the German people alone. He would receive the virginal purity of their fear in its full power.

We proceeded to the second town without incident. The second town was an exact replica of the first, with the white bedsheets hanging from every window, and the frightened people lined up along the street to watch us come in. We stopped again, and there was Major Pusey strutting about, conferring loudly with the officers, making flamboyant gestures, trying to salvage what he could out of a bad situation, theatrically speaking. But he had made up his mind. He came back to the jeep and told Brierly, "Pull out in front." Brierly carefully maneuvered the jeep past all the vehicles until we were in front of the tanks. Then he stopped.

Pusey stood up in the jeep, with his back to the tanks, raised his right arm, and gave a decisive "Forward!" signal and we were off. Soon we were out in open country.

I was seething with resentment. To ride ahead of the tanks was madness. I felt excruciatingly exposed. This asshole was putting my life at risk to satisfy his vanity.

This ride came at a particularly bad time for me. For a couple of weeks now the certainty had been growing within me that I was going to be killed. The picture I kept seeing was always the same. I would be riding in a jeep and the jeep would be hit by an 88, a direct hit, everybody in the jeep blown to bits. I played a game with myself. As I was being driven about in the back seat of the jeep, I would pick out a landmark off in the distance to my left, it had to be on the left, a farmhouse, a church steeple, a big tree, and I would think, "Before I get to that farmhouse, I'm going to be killed," and I would sit back, stop breathing, my heart pounding, and wait for my death. When I reached the farmhouse, I would start breathing again.

So many 88s had fallen near me that I was convinced I had exhausted my allotment of luck. The shells couldn't miss me forever. The laws of probability said that wasn't possible.

The mountains we were in had modest elevations. We went over a crest and started down. At the bottom of this incline was a trough and then we would immediately start climbing again. At the top of the up side ahead, on the left, was a barn. "I'm going to get it before I reach that barn," I said to myself.

We went down the incline. We reached the bottom, the trough. Suddenly ahead of us and to the right, there was a *whomp!* A Nebelwerfer. Brierly came to a panic stop and he and Pusey jumped out of the jeep and raced for a deep ditch running alongside the road.

I scrambled out of the back seat. It took me longer to get out because I had to go out the front passenger's side. By the time I got out of the jeep, it was too late to make it to the ditch. I could hear the approaching whine of the second Nebelwerfer as it rushed through the air. I dove under the jeep. Good thing I had taken the bulky radio off my back when we first started out. I wouldn't have fit under the jeep with it on.

Whomp!

Oh, Jesus, that was close!

The Nebelwerfers were not as feared as the 88s but in one respect they were even scarier. The 88s came at you one at a time. The Nebelwerfers were rockets that came at you six at a time. If the first one landed in your vicinity, you had to sweat out five more coming in the same area, each one a second or two apart, and you knew they were already in the sky, coming at you. It was unbearable, waiting. The first one might miss you. The second one might miss you. The third one might miss you. The fourth one might miss you. The fifth one might miss you. But the sixth one might get you.

These six missed us. I got out from under the jeep and Brierly and Pusey dashed back. I was gratified to see that Pusey was pale and shaken. The man was all of a piece.

"Get this thing out of here!" he yelled at Brierly.

The strike force had halted. Brierly made a U-turn and we zoomed past everybody back to the end of the procession. After a few minutes of waiting, Pusey gave the command over my radio to proceed and we started off again.

Major Pusey never went to the head of the strike force again. He was content to be last in line. I appreciated his newly found prudence. Well, he was normally prudent. It was just that this one time he had had a fleeting case of MacArthur Vainglorious, as it is known to students of psychiatry, a mental condition characterized by pathological self-importance.

III

THE READER

Every week the battalion received one copy of *Time* magazine. This was the wartime overseas edition of *Time*. It was smaller in dimensions than the domestic *Time* and had fewer pages. The one copy was delivered to the officers at battalion CP and placed on the table.

I cannot overstate how important this *Time* was to me. Each week I looked forward to reading it with the excitement and anticipation of a kid waiting for a present at Christmas. I read every word of it. I was starved for news. My only other source of news, *Stars and Stripes,* confined itself pretty much to war news, what was happening on the various fronts all over the world. And while this was important and I read it zealously, it did not satisfy my hunger for news. I was interested in political developments, both domestic and international. I wanted to know what was happening in sports, movies, plays, books, medicine. I wanted to know which important people had died and the scandals involved in the divorces of the famous or the notorious. I wanted to know how many days Tommy Manville's latest bride had stayed with him before fleeing and seeking a lawyer. I wanted to stay connected to that world. I could only do that with *Time.*

Was the overseas *Time* edited by the same people who edited the domestic *Time?* Did the overseas *Time* employ the famous *Time* style? I wish I could remember. Did they describe a short man they liked as "diminutive" and a short man they didn't like as "shrimpy"? Did they call the same man "a friend" in one instance and "a crony" in another, depending on whether his companion was a Republican or a Democrat? Did they end stories with snappy, improbable quotes from unlikely mouths? "Said a Bulgarian peasant, 'It's just like hitting a hole in one.'"

The latest *Time* was on the table at battalion CP. Like a dog eyeing a steak, I kept my eye on it, but like a dog, innocently. It wouldn't do just to pick it up and read it. That would have been thought presumptuous of me. So I just waited patiently. Eventually the officers would bed down and I would be left alone with it, or practically alone.

None of the officers were readers. They would pick it up, idly flip through the pages, look at a picture or two, then put it down.

By two in the morning things had quieted down for the night. I still had the receiver to my ear but there was no radio traffic. Most of the officers were lying on the floor, under their blankets, sleeping. Two officers were left at the table, Major Pusey and Captain Bacovitch, who was S-3, Operations. I liked Bacovitch. He was a decent guy and I liked his broad Slavic features.

I figured it was time to make my move. The *Time* had lain undisturbed on the table for several hours. I quietly got up from my place at the end of the table and sidled along unobtrusively till I came to the *Time* and nonchalantly picked it up and slipped back to my chair.

I had read about two sentences when I heard Major Pusey bark with irritation in his voice, "Where's that *Time* magazine gone to?"

"Here you are, sir," I said cheerily and went over and handed it to him. He gave me an unfriendly look.

He opened it and glanced at a few pages and then after a minute or two, set it down at the far end of the table away from me.

He was telling me, "Hands off. This is for officers only."

Eat it, you prick, you.

Thank God for the mind. It's the only place where we have freedom of speech.

IV
THE NONFRATERNIZER

I was sitting in the jeep all by myself. The jeep was parked on the side of the road. Major Pusey was inside the battalion CP. I didn't know where Brierly had gone to.

Three Frenchmen came walking down the road toward me. They were talking excitedly in French. Each man carried a huge pack on his back, higher than his head, blankets, clothes, kitchen utensils, stuff like that.

The three were slave labor, conscripted from France to work on German farms. This was their first day of freedom. They had been liberated today by my battalion. They were on their way back to France, willing to walk home if that was what was required. In this area there was also Italian and Polish farm slave labor. It was strange. When the French were liberated, they set out immediately, that day, for home. The Italians, no. They made no move to leave. I wondered, were the Italians slave labor or had they come of their own free will? Or were conditions in Italy so bad they were not in a rush to get back there?

The three Frenchmen were so joyful it was a lovely thing to see. I motioned for them to come over to my jeep.

"Where are you going?" I asked in French.

"Home, of course!" they cried in unison.

"How long have you been here?"

The guy in the middle seemed to be their spokesman.

"Five years," he said, holding up five fingers.

"Did they feed you well?"

"Badly," he said, making a face.

But all three looked pretty healthy, sturdy, not malnourished at all.

I pulled out my pack of cigarettes. I gave them each a cigarette. They were expressive in their gratitude, but they did not smoke them. They saved them.

I had two cigarettes left in my pack. I gave the pack to the spokesman.

"Share them," I said.

But how he was going to share two cigarettes among three people, I had no idea.

Just then Major Pusey came out of the CP. The second he spotted the three by the jeep, he yelled angrily at me, "Stop talking to those people!"

"*Bonne chance*," I said hastily to them.

They immediately understood the situation but I could tell by the bewildered look on their faces that they didn't understand the reason for Pusey's anger. They walked away.

Pusey came up to me.

"You've been told not to have conversations with these people and the reason for it, haven't you?"

"Yes, sir," I said.

"We don't fraternize with the enemy!"

"Yes, sir."

"Then why do you do it?"

They're French, not German, you dumb ass. But I knew that if I told him they were French, it wouldn't make any difference. Any foreign language made Pusey uneasy.

"Try to act like a soldier, for God's sake," he said disgustedly.

"Yes, sir."

The no-talking edict was hard on me but I don't know if Pusey was really concerned about fraternization. It annoyed him to hear the sounds of German. He was fearful and suspicious of any non-English language.

One day I was on duty at battalion CP. There was a timid knock on the door. I didn't see any officer getting off his ass so I went to the door.

It was a frail old woman.

Haltingly, she asked for permission to bury her husband, who had just died.

Hearing the dreaded sounds of German, Major Pusey rushed to the door.

"Why are these people hanging around here?" he yelled accusingly at me as if I was the reason these people were hanging around here.

"*Raus mit!*" he roared at her, and she drew back, frightened and distraught.

He slammed the door shut.

But in all fairness to Major Pusey, he could be flexible and understanding with the natives. In one town we came to a mansion, the finest home I had yet seen in France or Germany. As they say in interior-decorating circles, the house was well appointed with fine furniture and paintings on the walls. Naturally this was the house the officers selected for battalion CP.

The resident in the house was a good-looking blonde of about forty. She had a great figure and spoke excellent English with the most beguiling accent. Beside that, because of her open and friendly manner, her vivacity, her good-natured laughter, she charmed the pants off the officers, in a manner of speaking, and none more so than Major Pusey. The officers hung around her like bashful schoolboys.

We had a rigid rule in the battalion. There could be no Germans living in the house that held the CP. But in this case an exception was made. She was allowed to have the second floor. We would stay downstairs. I caught Major Pusey going up the stairs behind her. He was laughing and she was giggling and he had his hand on her ass, squeezing it. But nothing happened. He came back in four or five minutes, not enough time. And the officers kept close tabs on each other so no one was going to have the opportunity to make her.

I looked at her and I thought, "This is one smart broad. She knows how to operate in a man's world."

She obviously was living a privileged life. How could she have prospered in Hitler's Germany if she wasn't a Nazi or didn't have Nazi connections?

V

THE HUNTER

We were going down a country road. I was in the back seat of the jeep with my radio. Brierly and Major Pusey were in the front. There were woods on both sides of us. No other vehicle was with us.

A deer came out of the woods on our left, ambled across the road in front of us, climbed the embankment, and then stopped, turning to look at us.

"Stop!" Pusey yelled.

Brierly jammed the brakes.

"Give me your gun! Quick!"

Brierly hurriedly handed him his carbine.

Pusey grabbed it, raised it, aimed, fired. The deer fell over backwards.

"Good shooting, sir!" Brierly cried out.

"I got him!"

Pusey was beaming.

He turned to look at me. His face was flushed, his eyes were bright. He wanted some praise. Nice going, you shithead, was the only praise he was going to get from me.

"I'd like to come back to these woods after the war and spend some time hunting," Pusey said. "I know there's a lot of game in here."

"You'd get plenty of it, sir, shooting like that!" Brierly said.

Pusey handed the carbine back to Brierly.

"Let's go," he said.

We left.

He hadn't gotten out of the jeep.

How unfathomable, to derive pleasure from killing.

VI

THE HORSEMAN

The helmet liner of General Patton had seventeen coats of lacquer. He was a two-gun man from the Wild West; he had a holster on each hip holding a pearl-handled Colt six-shooter. He carried a riding crop with him wherever he went. These were all stage props for he was part-general and part-actor. But he was an influential model. I can attest to that. I saw with my own eyes General Patton's effect on Major Pusey.

Major Pusey received an invitation to go back to Third Army Headquarters and have a drink with General Patton. It would not be a cozy tête-à-tête. Many other battalion commanders had also been invited, but that did not lessen the impact of the invitation.

Major Pusey was overcome. He was jubilant. He was thrilled and excited beyond bearing. He was walking ten feet above the ground. At last he would meet the great man. General Patton was his idol and a man destined for the history books. And he, Major Pusey, was going to be in his company. For one day, while he was with Patton, Major Pusey would be part of that history.

Finally the much-anticipated day came. Major Pusey went and returned like a little kid who had shared a hot dog with Babe Ruth. He was radiant. He referred to General Patton as "the Old Man" with an affectionate intimacy as if they had known each other for years. He spoke with little chuckling asides about idiosyncrasies of "the Old Man." He talked about him the way you would of your kindly old grandfather, amused by his eccentricities, yet proud of him. "He's quite a fellow," he would say with a faraway look on his face, as if he were remembering some intimate moment he had shared with the general.

Then he turned cold serious.

"But I'll tell you this. He's a great man. The minute he walks into a room, you know it, just the way he carries himself. He commands with every gesture he makes. He commands with just a look. Believe me, you know you're in the presence of a great man."

As soon as he got back, Major Pusey called all the officers in the battalion together at our CP. I was there with my radio.

He had been privy to command decisions made at the highest level. He had knowledge of a secret plan no less. But this was the brotherhood of high command. No second lieutenants were allowed in here, but he could tantalize them.

"I'm not at liberty to discuss this with you," he said in a solemn tone, "but something big is going to happen. It will end the war sooner than you might think. And I can assure you, we'll be very much involved in it. That's as much as I can tell you at this time."

What the big plan was, I never found out. As far as I was concerned, it continued to be business as usual.

For weeks afterwards, Major Pusey kept coming back to his visit.

"When I had a drink with the Old Man, he said to me . . . ."

"As you know, I spent some time with the Old Man. He's an amazing fellow—" followed by a chuckle.

About a week after his visit, Major Pusey suddenly showed up at the CP with a riding crop. Where he got it, I don't know. But Brierly had gone back to Regiment the day before. Probably Brierly had picked it up for him. Regiment could get you things.

And now Major Pusey was never parted from his riding crop. Wherever he went, it went. It was always in his hand. He would tap it annoyingly on the surface of the table at the CP. When he stood up, he would flick it gently across the calf of his right leg. He no longer just walked; he strode brandishing the goddamn thing. Sitting in the jeep, he held it in his hand across his lap. It might have come in handy if we had ever come across a horse that wasn't dead.

"Where's your fuckin' horse, Major?" I wanted to snarl at him.

His riding crop irritated me no end. Every time I saw him with it, which was all the time, it irritated me. I guess maybe it was the class thing: I have a country manor and stables and you don't. When someone comes at me waving a riding crop, my collective unconscious kicks in and my peasant blood comes rushing up. "What the hell do you intend to do with that thing? Who are you going to whip?"

Major Pusey was emulating General Patton, and who had General Patton been emulating? Probably some upper-class British officer named Chidley he had observed in the First World War when he was young and impressionable.

It went beyond irritation. I deeply resented the riding crop. I was offended. I didn't care what General Patton did. He was so far back it didn't matter what he did. If he wanted to wear spurs, let him. But it was different here. We were at the front. Men were being killed or maimed almost on a daily basis. Out of respect for them, there was no place here for theatrical play-acting, for posturing. It was an affront to the memory of the dead.

I began to fantasize about destroying the riding crop. One afternoon Major Pusey stepped out of the CP and left the riding crop on the table. There was no one else in the CP. I was alone with it. I eyed it. I could go over there and break it in half and leave the two pieces on the table for him to find. But it would be smarter just to hide it. Then I could profess my innocence and swear up and down I hadn't seen it. But that wouldn't fool anybody. And what if they searched the place and found it?

But as much as I wanted to do something, I knew I wouldn't. As much as I hated that riding crop, it wasn't worth my life. If I did something, I would be asking for a one-way ticket to a rifle company. Then instead of being at battalion CP listening to messages from a rifle-company radio operator, I would be a rifle-company radio operator sending messages to battalion. Or, worse yet, they would take my radio from me and stick a rifle in my hands.

So it wasn't worth it. Keep your riding crop, Major Pusey, you horse's ass.

16

The Rear

WE TOOK THE TOWN and then stayed put. Elements of an armored division relieved us. Without us even being aware of it, the front gradually became the rear because the armored division pushed the war away from us. The change kind of snuck up on us. The first inkling we had that we were now the rear came when we got the news—"The Red Cross girls will be at the town square at eleven o'clock this morning to hand out coffee and doughnuts." Word of their coming spread like wildfire from house to house.

Everybody was going.

It was partly the coffee and doughnuts, of course, or just doughnuts for me, but there was a lot more to it than that. The guys hadn't seen any American girls for months and months. I hadn't seen any since I left the States. We were homesick for American girls.

We had seen a steady procession of European women, specifically peasant women. They were little better than beasts of burden on the farms. Just this morning I had seen one in action. She came to the town pump to get water. She had two huge wooden buckets, one each at the end of a pole. She filled them and then with little apparent effort, swung the pole up on her shoulders and walked off. I knew that no Red Cross girl would have been strong enough to carry one of those buckets, much less two. As far as that went, I couldn't have gotten that pole up off the ground myself. But this woman, so typical of her class, was a woman in name only. Stolid, as expressionless as an ox, with legs like tree trunks, and a torso like Two-Ton Tony Galento's, she had no curves. We were more than ready to see another kind of woman.

And it was not lust that drew us. We didn't go to ogle the Red Cross girls and indulge in lecherous fantasies. I didn't think such a thing was possible but my sex drive had left me since I joined the outfit. I quit having sudden and unbidden erections. I quit having sexual thoughts day and night. I quit having wet dreams. I had something else on my mind—survival. When I thought of a girl now, it was not the sexual part I dwelt on. I remembered instead her softness of manner, how she had touched my cheek or my hair. I remembered the tenderness, not the passion.

In the barracks in the States, the talk had been mostly about sex, with guys recounting the sexual adventures they had on their last pass. At the front there was no talk of women and sex. It was as if everyone had taken a vow of celibacy. There were no dirty jokes either. It was really quite amazing.

So we went and the girls were perfect. They weren't flirty or provocative or aloof, just sweet. There were three of them. They were dressed in military clothing, O.D. shirt and pants and a field jacket. Their hair shone. Their teeth were sparkling white. They had just enough make-up on, not too much; their lips were just red enough.

We stood quietly and stared at them as they worked, bustling about, serving everybody. We looked on, appreciating every smile, every gesture, every hand to the hair, every step. They were everything we were hoping they would be. They were beautiful, slim, clean, fresh, cheerful, alert, spirited, confident, responsive, intelligent. They were full of life, full of fun. They were uniquely American girls. They reminded us of a world we had left behind and now saw a glimpse of again.

"I wonder if they put out," Groton said. "What do you think, Charley?"

"Who knows?" I said.

"If they put out, it won't be to one of us," Jelich said. "It'll be to an officer."

"I saw a whore in England spread her legs on the sidewalk and piss standing up," Hillbilly said. "She wasn't wearing anything under her skirt."

"What's that got to do with anything?" Jelich said, disgusted. Hillbilly was polluting the moment.

"I just happened to think of it, that's all," Hillbilly said defensively.

The second occurrence providing evidence that we were the rear was the Army showed us a movie.

The first we heard about it was when Jelich popped in and said, "There's a movie tonight in the anti-tank barn, seven o'clock."

This was great news. I hadn't seen a movie since I left the States and I knew the fellows hadn't seen one in months either.

The anti-tank guys didn't live in the barn. They lived in the house but the barn was in their yard. There was no building in town large enough to accommodate everybody in a single sitting, so we would see the movie on a staggered schedule, unit by unit.

"What's the movie?" somebody asked.

"I don't know," Jelich said. "They said it was a musical. That's all I know."

Oh, shit. A musical. I hated silly-assed musicals, with their childish plots, lousy acting, ridiculous chorus numbers, tuneless songs, and dumb dialogue. What I wanted to see was a serious drama or even a good mystery, something you could immerse yourself in, something that would absorb you, something that would help you forget where you were even if it was only for a couple of hours.

Would it be an old movie with Carmen Miranda or Alice Faye? Or would it be a new one, with somebody like Betty Grable? Yes, that's what I expected, Betty Grable. Would it be about Tin Pan Alley? Would it be about Hollywood's favorite occupation, show business?

The last movie I saw was a musical. The girl I was with had her heart set on seeing it and I wasn't about to say no. I was positioning myself for a reward later on that never came.

Just before seven o'clock, we climbed up the ladder into the barn's hayloft and made ourselves comfortable in the loose hay. The white screen was down at one end of the loft. The projectionist was behind us, setting up.

The movie started.

The first thing I saw was: *Republic Pictures Presents* . . . .

Was this a joke? A Republic picture? What happened to all the good pictures from Twentieth-Century Fox? From Metro-Goldwyn-Mayer? From Paramount? They were going to give us a piece of shit from Republic. This was insufferable. Here were men risking their lives for their country and the best the Army could do was show them a Republic picture. For sure some of the guys up here in the hayloft, this might be the last movie they would see on this earth. Didn't they deserve better? It showed the contempt the Army had for the infantry. They thought we were a bunch of morons who wouldn't know the difference.

Republic didn't make musicals. Republic made cowboy pictures. I was an expert on Republic's output because I was a connoisseur of cowboy pictures. When I was a kid, I spent every Saturday afternoon at the tiny Allen Theatre, before it burned down, on Acushnet Avenue near Coffin Avenue, watching a cowboy picture. And not just a cowboy picture, because to beat its competition, the Allen showed three pictures on Saturday afternoon, instead of the usual two, plus a chapter picture, which was what we called serials. You went in the theater at one-thirty to get a good seat and then it started at two o'clock and lasted until six o'clock and you came out bleary-eyed.

I saw all the cowboys, mostly from Monogram or Republic. I didn't see Tom Mix because he had stopped making pictures. My No. 2 favorite was the muscular Buck Jones. My No. 1 favorite was the lean and darkly handsome Tom Tyler. I was familiar with the lack of quality in Republic pictures. Later I read that Republic sometimes shot a cowboy picture in one week.

The opening credits finished and the story started. My sense of foreboding was well founded. This was probably the worst movie ever made. They must have made it on a budget of five hundred dollars.

The leading lady and man were singing in front of a white picket fence. Behind the fence was an ivy-covered cottage and a big rosebush. There was a full moon in the sky. Now MGM would have had a real picket fence and a real cottage. Republic had a canvas backdrop with the scene painted on it, the white picket fence, the rosebush, the ivy-covered cottage, and the full moon. The duo was singing in front of a piece of canvas. The thing was that the painting was so bad, so crude, so amateurish, so rudimentary, so poorly done, it wouldn't have fooled a two-year-old.

The leading lady had no voice.

"She's fucking the director," Groton whispered in my ear. "That's how she got the part."

I wasn't sure she was fucking the director. She was long in the tooth and not particularly attractive. In an MGM musical, she would have been the heroine's aunt and kept in the background.

The leading man had a gigolo mustache. His acting was wooden, his gestures stiff.

The men watched the film silently and intently. There were no wisecracks. How desperate they were for entertainment that this film could entertain them! And how differently the audience would have responded if this had been shown in a college town. Then you wouldn't have been able to hear the actors' lines, there would have been so many attempted witticisms yelled out by the collegians.

But I had to admit the film did have a certain perverse attraction. It was so bad that I was fascinated by it. To think that some people actually made this film, wrote the lines, dressed the actors, painted the canvases.

The film suddenly snapped and broke. The projectionist set about rethreading it. Everybody stirred a bit.

Jimmy Moura, my Portagee buddy from Taunton, was sitting next to me. He was the battalion's switchboard operator. He said to me, "You know what I'd like right now, Charley?"

"No, what?"

"A linguiça sandwich. I'd take a big fork and a big piece of linguiça and I'd hold the linguiça just above the flames and when that linguiça got hot, the skin would split open and the juices would start running and they'd sizzle when they hit the flames and when the linguiça was hot all the way through, I'd grab a big chunk of Portagee bread and slap the linguiça in it and all those hot juices would make the bread turn orange and then I'd take a big bite. Oooh! Did you ever taste anything so delicious?"

"No, I never have," I said and I meant it.

We were all sitting in the hay. Moura lay down and laid his head on my lap.

"I'm going to pretend you're a girl," he said and closed his eyes.

I stroked his hair gently.

"That feels good," he said. "How about going steady?"

"I'm already spoken for," I said.

The film started whirring again and Moura sat up.

The third occurrence providing evidence that we were the rear was the AMG (Allied Military Government) came to town.

"You want to keep me company?" Jelich said to me.

"Sure. Why not?"

I had nothing better to do.

I followed him out into the street.

"Where are we going?"

"I want to try and find some stamps to send my kid brother. He's a stamp collector."

We went to the house where the *Bürgermeister* had his offices.

"There should be some here," Jelich said. "He's going to get a lot of mail."

The house had suffered shell damage and had been abandoned. We went in and walked up the stairs. The *Bürgermeister*'s office was on the second floor of the two-storied house. He had the room facing the street. The top of the stairs was right by the door to his office.

The office was wide open; the door had been blown off. The office was in total disarray, chairs upside down, the floor covered with all kinds of books and papers and letters.

I sat down on the floor by the top of the stairs and stretched out my legs and relaxed. Jelich sat in the doorway of the *Bürgermeister*'s office. We faced each other.

It was a clear, crisp day. Above me was the sky, a beautiful blue today. A shell, either one of ours or one of theirs, had blown the roof off. I felt the direct warmth of the sun. It felt good.

Jelich had a bundled bunch of opened letters on his lap. He had brought along a pair of scissors. He would take one letter, remove the contents from the envelope, neatly cut out the upper right-hand corner of the envelope where the stamp was, then put the contents back in the envelope, and go on to the next one. He was painstaking but fast. Pretty soon he had a nice little pile of stamps on the floor.

I wondered how his brother would get the glued paper off the back of the stamps. Didn't stamp collectors just want the stamp by itself?

"I haven't seen my kid brother in three years," Jelich said. "I'm afraid he's going to forget what I look like."

"How old is he?"

"Twelve. He was nine when I left. I'm the oldest, he's the youngest. I always kind of had a soft spot for him."

I heard feet thumping up the stairs. Somebody was coming. I looked. It was a major. He had AMG painted in big white letters across his helmet and an AMG armband. I stared at him. He was good-looking as all get out, square-jawed, a face selected by Hollywood casting. He was an officer dandy. He looked like he had stepped out of a bandbox. He was immaculate. It was astonishing to see anyone this clean out here. His O.D. pants had a razor-sharp crease and fit too snugly to be government issue. They had to be tailor-made or tailor-altered. In fact, all of his clothing was formfitting, which again suggested a tailor. He was wearing paratrooper boots and they were shined to a fare-thee-well. Mirrorlike, they threatened to blind you with reflected light if you looked at them too long. Clearly, he was a man who had connections. He had access to a tailor, a dry cleaner, a presser, a shoe-shine boy, a shower.

"What are you doing here, soldier?" he demanded of me, frowning, his voice full of suspicion.

I looked at him blankly. What could I say? I'm sitting on my ass, sir, getting some sun? That didn't seem like a good answer so I said nothing. But I was blocking his way. I swung my legs over to let him by.

He came up by me and then he saw Jelich with the letters on his lap.

"What are you doing?" he asked Jelich.

I could tell from the shock in his voice and his open mouth that this was not going to be good.

"I'm getting some stamps for my kid brother," Jelich said.

"Don't you know there are regulations against looting? I could have you court-martialed for this!" he said sharply.

Jelich just looked at him.

"Those are records we have to go through! You two get out of here and don't come back here again! This building is off limits to you!"

The pile of cut stamps was on the floor by Jelich. He started to scoop them up to put in his pocket.

"Leave those!" the major yelled. "That's government property! Don't touch them!"

He was in quite a state.

We got up and left silently. Once on the street, Jelich muttered, "We took this town. You'd think they'd show us a little appreciation."

About an hour later, Jelich and I were in our house. We heard a commotion outside. We went to the window to see what was going on.

Outside in the street was the AMG major. He had his translator with him. The translator, a sergeant, was a Jewish refugee from Germany. He had fled Germany in the 1930s as a victim and returned in 1945 as a victor. Did that give him any satisfaction? It would have me.

In front of the major was a semicircle of six or seven German men. They stood before him like schoolboys, caps in hand, bowing and scraping, vigorously nodding assent to everything he was saying or what the translator said he was saying. I recognized the *Bürgermeister* among them. Maybe the other guys were the Town Council.

The major was laying the law down.

"Look at him!" Jelich said scornfully. "Look at him lord it over these people!"

Jelich was in a dark mood. He was brooding over the loss of the stamps. That the major had popped up outside our very window was an unfortunate coincidence.

"He's in his glory now," Jelich said bitingly. "This is what he lives for. Look at him stick out his jaw. Look at him puff up his chest. He thinks he's Mussolini."

The major was not being friendly to the Germans, not that I held it against him. Why should we be pals with these people? Look at the misery and death they had brought upon much of Europe.

"Now he's holding up his fingers," Jelich continued. "No. 1, you can't do this. No. 2, you can't do that. No. 3, you can't do this. No. 4, you can't do that. No. 5, you can't do this."

In *A Bell for Adano* the AMG officer was teaching the Italians about democracy. I guess that was what this AMG major was doing. He was teaching the Germans about democracy in a manner they would understand.

"I wish an 88 would come over right now," Jelich said. "I'd like to see him dive headfirst into that mud puddle. We'll see how good you look then. Ooh, did you get a spot on your pants, sir? Here, use this lighter fluid to get it off. Oh, you mean your whole pants are muddy? Well, in that case, sir, let them dry in the sun and then scrape it off. Yeah. I'd like to see him face down in the mud, saying his prayers. Give him a taste of it. See how he likes it."

I laughed.

"I can see him after the war, lying through his teeth," Jelich said. "He's in an English pub and he says, 'Yes, sometimes it was touch-and-go. We'd go into a town and Jerry would be at one end of the town and we'd be at the other end, setting up the government.'"

The fourth occurrence providing evidence that we were the rear was I saw a war correspondent. He was wearing a trench coat. No self-respecting war correspondent would be caught in anything but a trench coat. That was their official uniform. I think what happened was that early in the war Hollywood made a movie about a foreign correspondent and he was a glamorous figure dashing about, escaping danger. The war correspondents saw the movie and liked the portrayal. It was the way they saw themselves. And the importance of this movie was that the hero was wearing a stylish trench coat. From that day on, all the war correspondents wore trench coats.

This war correspondent was a short, plump man. I was walking down the street and he was coming toward me. He had a sandy mustache. He was eating a candy bar. His face had broken out with zits. Probably too many sweets. Chocolate will do that to you.

He was stuffing the candy bar into his mouth. His cheeks were puffed out with it. He was gobbling it down as fast as he could. He reminded me of when I was a kid. We had one kid in our gang who had enough money to buy candy bars and he would gobble them down as fast as he could before anybody could ask him for a bite. I was too fastidious myself to ask him for one.

The war correspondent didn't look at me as he came by but I got a good look at the candy bar. It looked like my favorite bar, a Powerhouse, long and swollen with a delicious mixture of chocolate, nuts, caramel, and nougat. My mouth watered looking at it. Where had he gotten a bar like that over here?

The fifth occurrence providing evidence that we were the rear was the MPs (Military Police) suddenly showed up. I was walking by the town square when I saw the first one. He was on the sidewalk, observing things. He was an imposing six-footer, broad-shouldered. He looked like an athlete. But the striking thing about him was not his physique but his expression. He looked like the Sheriff of Abilene or Dodge City and he wanted you to know this was his town and he was more than capable of handling the cowboys who were coming to town to raise hell. He looked you in the eye challengingly with an unpleasant smile on his face. He stood there with his broad shoulders, straight as a ramrod, perfect military posture. His clean-cut presence of manly vigor was a reproach to us. We slunk by, narrow-shouldered, hunched over, scrawny, pallid, dirty, unkempt—America's fighting men.

The word went out. "Don't go outside without a helmet. You're liable to get fined."

This was a startling warning. I had never heard it before. Nobody had to tell you to wear a helmet at the front. In fact, sometimes you wished you had two helmets to put on. Even the dumbest of soldiers knew you risked getting a chunk of shrapnel in your skull if you weren't wearing a helmet and maybe even if you were.

But this town was out of it. You could have gone outside with just a hair net on and your head would not have been at risk. So this warning was perplexing. Was this Patton-ordered fine militarily justified to keep the troops at the ready or was it a charade, designed to give pretend warriors the thrill of pretend danger?

So now we had fines. How long would it be before we had to start saluting officers? Civilization was moving in on us.

Whenever we were relieved and put in Regimental Reserve or whatever, the cycle was always the same. The first day there was an enormous sense of relief. You had made it. There were high spirits, euphoria, giddy silliness. But after that high point, the euphoria began to dissipate. By the third day it was gone, replaced by a gnawing anxiety. When do we go back? And with every passing day, you knew you were that much closer to the dreaded command, "Load up!"

That was why our best protection was when one of our rifle companies was badly shot up. Division would not send us into action with a company that was way below strength. A company in pitiful shape was our security. We watched vigilantly for the coming of replacements. As long as no replacements showed up, things could not have looked better. But when some truckloads of replacements rolled in, that was a gloomy day. It meant that now there was no reason why we couldn't go back in.

But in this town where we rested, we were at full strength. There was no question we would have been happy to stay here until the end of the war. We were safe here. Nobody wanted to go back.

But I noticed a peculiar thing about the men. The euphoria was gone. The anxiety was gone. But they didn't seem to be enjoying themselves. In fact, I sensed a growing irritability among them that they had never exhibited before. I pondered this change. Why? What had happened? The only answer I could come up with was: the encroachments of civilization.

There is something deeply disturbing about civilization. It makes you edgy.

It was crazy and perverse but I think a little part of us regretted being here. Something was slipping away from us. Soon we would be like everybody else, subject to the everyday cant of living. When we were at the front, we were down to essentials. At the front we were special. We were alone. Nobody wanted to be there with us. At the front there were no Red Cross girls, no movies, no AMG officers, no war correspondents, no MPs. We were the Chosen Few. We were like lepers. Nobody voluntarily steps onto an island of lepers. And in our leperdom, in our aloneness, there was a brotherhood, a purity. We were losing that purity in this town and I think in some deep recess of our being, we knew it. At the front we were the most ourselves. At the front we were the most the best in ourselves.

17

Captain Baker

BRUNO (THAT WAS HIS FIRST NAME) was a mysterious figure in the battalion. He flitted about, now you see him, now you don't. He would disappear for days. Where was he? What was he doing? I don't know. He was like me, at the very bottom, a private, but he didn't seem to answer to anybody. Another strange thing about him—he didn't carry a weapon.

If you looked at the roster to find his MOS (Military Occupational Specialty), what would it say? I have no idea. The closest I can come to describing his function is to say he was a jack-of-all-trades for the battalion staff officers. He had the free use of a jeep and ran errands for them, going back to Regiment regularly. It was he who delivered Lieutenant Tidwell's packages to Regiment on their first leg back to the States.

He was an excellent barber. He would cut the officers' hair. He didn't cut the enlisted men's hair. There were too many of us. We had to cut each other's hair, with sometimes comical results.

He was a marvelous cook. I had no firsthand knowledge of this but I gathered from what Sergeant Drummond told me that on certain occasions Bruno would cook special meals for the officers. He would go back to Regiment and get flavorful foods and delicacies, such as our kitchen never saw. It wasn't chipped beef on toast or hash or pork and beans. Of course, these small, intimate dinners were never prepared when we were involved in an engagement. Things were much too hectic then. But when we were resting up, that was when they took place. Apparently Bruno's culinary skills were on a level far above that of our cooks. If they were cooks, then he was a chef. This didn't surprise me too much, for anger born from unhappiness cannot bring out the best in food, and Army cooks seemed universally unhappy. Were they unwilling students at Cooks and Bakers School? Sometimes when you got in line and held out your mess kit to a cook for him to spoon or spatula something into it, he gave you a look like he'd rather kill you than feed you.

The officers very much appreciated Bruno's way with food and one day I saw why.

We were in a town. Outside the town was open ground and then a river. The objective was to occupy all the ground between the town and the river, that is, clear the area of German infantry, push them back across the river. For a whole day there was fighting. Then the second day began with more of the same. By midafternoon of the second day, the objective had been achieved. The strain was now off the officers. I was on duty at battalion CP, a large room in a house. Things were winding down but that didn't mean I would be parting from my radio anytime soon. Alertness had to be maintained at all times.

During the entire engagement I had been on duty at the CP. I hadn't eaten anything the first day. I hadn't eaten anything the second day up to now. That's a long time to go without eating, but I was not consciously hungry. That feeling soon passes. I felt light-headed and weak but that was all. I was lucky. In this instance physical exertion was not required of me. All I had to do was sit there with my handset to my ear. That made the lack of food much easier to take.

I could have opened a K ration but this I declined to do. I preferred going without sustenance until I could get a decent, hot meal. I couldn't eat a K ration. God knows, I did my best. The last time I tried I took a bite of some canned cheese compound. I actually held it in my mouth. I moved it to the entrance of my throat. There it lay, poised to go down. But that was as far as I could take it. I could not swallow it. I could not make it go down.

K rations were absolutely the most inedible, the most unappetiz-ing, the most horrible concoctions of so-called food products ever processed. Some criminal enterprise must have bribed Army pro-curement agents.

Bruno was in the vicinity of the CP. There were some stairs that led up from the CP room. I had caught glimpses of Bruno going up and down these stairs but I hadn't paid any attention to him. I had no idea what he was up to.

And now while the officers were relaxing, Bruno suddenly ap-peared on the bottom step.

"Chow's on!" Bruno called out.

As one man, the officers jumped up and went single file up the stairs. They reappeared shortly. Each one carried a cup of coffee and a heaping plate of heavenly smelling, mouth-watering food, a feast. There was crisp, golden-brown roast chicken, a large, steaming baked potato cut in halves the long way with a generous coating of butter, bright yellow kernels of corn, soft, freshly baked biscuits. I hadn't seen a meal like this since I left the States.

The officers sat down at the table and proceeded to eat with gusto. Everybody was in a good mood. There was a lot of joking back and forth.

I tried not to look at their plates out of good manners. But I was embarrassed for them. How could they eat in front of me? Hadn't I been here with them all through this engagement? Hadn't they seen me here all through the first day? Hadn't they seen me here all through the night sitting at this table awake and on duty while they slept? Hadn't they seen me here all day today? How could they not see me now? How could they not offer me a plate? I was the only en-listed man at the CP. Couldn't they spare one plate?

They finished eating and pushed the empty plates away and sat there, enjoying that full feeling. One of the officers stacked up the dirty plates and carefully carried them back up the stairs to Bruno.

After about thirty minutes, Captain Baker came in from the field. He looked utterly spent, exhausted. He smiled and nodded at me. He always did that. He always acknowledged my presence. I liked Cap-tain Baker.

Once he was walking ahead of me going into the CP. He held the door open and stepped aside, gesturing for me to go in first. Unbelievable. "Thank you, sir," I said.

Captain Baker was not in the infantry. But his job was just as dangerous as a rifleman's. He was a forward observer in the field artillery, the only one assigned to our battalion. He was on the line with the rifle companies, on the lookout for targets. He had his own radio operator, a sergeant in the artillery. They were a team. They moved around together. They used a different frequency from mine but occasionally they had trouble getting through to the fire center and I would help by relaying their firing data back to the rear. I marveled at how calmly Captain Baker would speak into his mouthpiece and give corrections. "One-fifty left, two hundred over," he would say matter-of-factly as if nothing was happening where he was lying.

I seldom saw him but when he came in the CP he was always pleasant with the other officers, even-tempered, quick to laugh. If you saw them together, you'd think his job was stress-free and theirs was not.

He was of medium height, not a big man. He had a small mustache. He wore glasses. He looked older than the other officers. They were mostly in their twenties. He looked to be in his thirties. Someone told me he had been a schoolteacher in civilian life but I don't know if that was true or not.

As Captain Baker walked in, one of the officers called to him.

"There's chow upstairs, Baker!"

"Good!" he said.

He immediately went up and came back with a plateful and coffee. He sat among the officers and ate.

"This is wonderful!" he said.

When he finished, he took the plate upstairs. He came back down the stairs.

He walked over to where I was sitting at the end of the table.

He stood by me.

"Have you eaten yet?" he said to me.

I was dumbfounded. I wasn't his responsibility. He had nothing to do with me. Yet he was interceding. He knew I hadn't eaten. He had taken in the whole situation at a glance. Some people know things intuitively and some don't. But what should I say? I didn't want to lie but I knew the other officers, who were watching and listening, didn't want me to eat. I didn't want to arouse their ire for fear they would stick it to me later. That was why I did not answer immediately. I was thinking a mile a minute. Should I tell him I wasn't hungry?

"No, sir. I haven't," I said.

"You go on up and get yourself a plate," he said. "Tell Bruno I said to give you a plate."

He was breaking the code, spoiling the help. He was going against the group. He was showing the other officers up and they wouldn't like it. But he went ahead and did it anyway. He didn't care. He was his own man, a rare thing.

"What about my radio, sir?"

"Don't worry about it. I'll take over for you."

And so saying, he sat down beside me, took my receiver, and put it to his ear. He sat there placidly.

I was deeply touched.

This is a man I could follow, I thought. But what good could I do him? He needed someone to help him spot targets, someone with the eyes of an eagle, not someone who saw blurs at a hundred yards.

I got up.

I went up the stairs.

Bruno was in an open room at the top of the stairs. It was a kitchen. He was standing by the stove. He was not happy to see me. A look of alarm came over his face when I walked in.

"Captain Baker said to give me a plate of food," I said firmly.

"I can't be feeding everybody," Bruno muttered with a scowl, but he reached for a clean plate. I know how he felt. Feeding an enlisted man was setting a bad precedent. But I was a little taken aback by his surliness. He had always been cordial to me before but, then again, I had never asked him for anything before.

There was a lot of food everywhere. There was a big pan of chicken and another of potatoes sitting on top of the stove. They were half full. There was no way he was going to run out of food. So why did he begrudge me one measly plate?

But I have to give Bruno credit. He didn't short me. He gave me a full plate with everything on it, including choice pieces of chicken. He cut the potato in half and put butter on it.

He handed me the plate.

"Thanks," I said.

I picked up the silverware. I didn't take any coffee.

I returned to Captain Baker and sat down beside him. I thought he might turn the handset back to me at this point, so that I could hold it to my ear with one hand and eat with my other hand, which would have been kind of hard because I really needed two hands to cut up the chicken and potato. But he made no move to hand me the receiver. He didn't even look at me. He just sat there placidly holding the receiver in place. Clearly he meant for me to eat, so eat I did.

It was the most delicious meal I ever had. I savored every morsel. I would have liked to eat slower, make the exquisite flavors last as long as possible, but I didn't want to impose on him, so I ate as fast as I could.

When I finished, I took the plate back up to the kitchen. Bruno turned away and wouldn't even look at me. It was clear he was still smoldering.

"It was delicious," I said to Bruno. I didn't say that to rub it in, although I could see he might take it that way. I meant it, but Bruno was in no mood to accept a compliment from me.

I went back down the stairs. I sat down again next to Captain Baker. He looked at me.

I looked him in the eye.

"Thank you, sir," I said and I didn't say it like we usually say thank you.

He smiled and nodded at me, handed me the receiver, and rejoined the officers at the other end of the table.

Two weeks later Captain Baker was dead. Moura saw the body. Captain Baker was stretched out just below the crest of a hill. Apparently he had been crawling to the top to observe what was on the other side.

"It looked like he was sleeping," Moura told me. "There wasn't a mark on him. I think the concussion from a Nebelwerfer got him."

He was a good man. May his soul rest in peace.

18

The Priest Protecting the Furniture

I **WAS LOUNGING AROUND** the house. Spumoni was sitting at the table, writing a letter home. I took out my scissors and started cutting my fingernails. When I finished, I took off my shoes and socks and started cutting my toenails. I was using a wonderful pair of scissors I had found in a house some time back. They were small, curved, and stamped *Mabruso, Solingen* (fifty-five years later I still use them to cut my nails). Spumoni and I were the only guys around.

When I got my shoes and socks back on, I noticed Spumoni was through writing and was just sitting there, staring off into space, with a big frown on his face.

"You look like you lost your best friend," I said.

He shook his head.

"I did something that's really been bothering me lately," he said in a low voice.

"What?"

He looked at me searchingly. Spumoni was such a brooding, serious guy I knew this had to be something big. There was no play in him.

He told me. When the outfit was fighting in France, before I joined them, one day he had been laying wire across this cemetery behind a Catholic church. Suddenly he felt terrible stomach cramps. He had the runs. He wanted to get to the road outside the cemetery but he knew he would never make it. He ripped open his pants where he stood and squatted.

"I've felt real bad about it ever since," he said.

"Why?" I said.

"It's a desecration of the dead."

"I don't think the dead minded too much," I said.

"It's not the dead I'm worried about. It's God."

Theological matters always tired my brain so I said nothing.

"I shouldn't have done it," he said.

"I don't see where you had much choice," I said. "It was either that or do it in your pants."

"I'm a Catholic."

"I know that."

"And it was in a Catholic cemetery," he said despondently. "That's what makes it so much worse."

Theology again.

"I shit on a Catholic grave. That's a sin. That's a bad sin. It's like a sacrilege. I think I'm going to be punished for it."

Oh, so that was what this was all about. The anger of the Catholic God. And what better way to punish Spumoni than by dropping an 88 on him? Spumoni was trying to figure out in his own mind the reason for the death he saw coming.

Just about then Hillbilly came in the house. He was terribly upset.

Next to our house was a pasture. In the pasture was a dead horse, close by the fence. As he came walking up, Hillbilly saw a dog eating off the dead horse. This enraged Hillbilly. He jumped the fence and aimed several vicious kicks at the dog but they all missed. The dog backed off and slunk away.

Hillbilly came in the house, angry and disturbed.

"I should have shot that dog," he said balefully. "He deserved to be shot."

"Maybe he was starving," Spumoni said.

Hillbilly gave him a dirty look.

"Henderson is waiting for you outside the CP," he told Spumoni. "He's going back to Regiment to pick up some stuff and he wants you to go with him."

"Why didn't he take you?" Spumoni said.

"I don't know. Ask him."

Hillbilly's day had started off badly and there was more to come. A few minutes after Spumoni left, there was a peremptory knock on the door. I got up to see who it was, but before I could get there, the door opened and this woman barged in.

This was her house. She was a tall, broad-shouldered woman. One would have thought her side had won the war. Her manner was imperious and scornful. I would have hated to have to work for her. That would not have been fun.

She was excited and voluble. She advanced into the room and unleashed a torrent of German at us. I managed to get the gist of what she was saying. She claimed we were scratching her furniture. There were marks on the table that hadn't been there before we moved in. We were damaging her furniture. This was pure bullshit. We hadn't put a single mark on her furniture. She was just sore because we had kicked her out of her home. Two days ago her people had been trying to kill us. It didn't put me in too good a mood to hear this.

Hillbilly was watching and listening to her with close attention. He kept trying to break in. "What's she saying? What's she saying?"

I waited until I was certain I had it right.

"She says we're damaging her furniture," I said.

"I've had enough of these goddamn Krauts!" Hillbilly exclaimed. "We're over here fighting because of them and she's got the goddamn nerve to complain about her furniture? Here, lady, I'll show you some goddamn damage!" he yelled at her. And so saying, he picked up one of the wooden chairs from the table and hurled it. It landed on its side and skidded to the other end of the room.

She screamed in outrage. She was apoplectic. I thought she might attack him.

"Come on! Get the hell out of here!" Hillbilly snarled. He grabbed her by the arm and propelled her toward the door. "You're lucky I don't burn your goddamn house down!"

Her tirade never let up.

He pushed her out the door and slammed the door shut. Then he opened it and yelled after her, "Don't come back here again!"

Now she was beside herself. We could hear her as she walked through the yard past our windows, a furious monologue, an unintelligible stream of German at the top of her lungs.

About twenty minutes later, she was back. She barged into the room again, this time accompanied by a priest. He stepped into the room behind her.

The priest was tall and thin. His complexion was sallow. He had several days' growth of beard. The front of his black cassock was rich with the greasy food stains of many meals. He was unkempt and dirty-looking. Like me, he looked as if he hadn't had a bath in a long time. This was one priest who would not have been welcome in a Bing Crosby priest picture.

This time the woman didn't say a word. She was going to let the priest do the talking. He spoke English and spoke it well.

"My dear sir," he said, "this dear lady has said that you are harming her furniture."

Hillbilly's eyes got big. He didn't need me to interpret this time. At long last he could confront an aggravation face-to-face.

"If it wasn't for you goddamn people, we wouldn't be here and you've got the goddamn gall to complain about some furniture?"

"My dear sir—" the priest began again.

"I'm tired of this shit!" Hillbilly cried. "Out!" He gestured with his arm toward the door. "Right now! Out! Out!"

Hillbilly put his arm across the priest's back and directed him firmly to the door, walking along with him to help him on his way.

"I shall report this to your commanding officer," the priest protested.

"Go ahead! While you're at it, why don't you report it to your commanding officer, Hitler?"

Hillbilly gave him a little push out the door. The woman followed silently behind. Hillbilly closed the door behind them.

I thought Hillbilly had a point. If this priest was really a man of God, that is to say, a hero, would not one of Hitler's prisons or worse have been his inevitable destination? How had he managed to survive in this house of evil except by saying the right things to his parishioners in his Sunday sermons? The doctors, the lawyers, the teachers, they all followed Hitler. Why should the priests and ministers be any different? Still, we expect more from them.

A good thing Spumoni hadn't been around to see Hillbilly manhandle the priest.

Now that they were outside, the woman and the priest gave vent to their feelings. They stood outside our windows, probably debating what to do next. The woman opened up her big Teutonic guns of outrage. The priest matched her, his high voice vibrating with indignation. The duet, clearly heard by us, was too much for Hillbilly.

"Goddamn it!" he said.

He bolted out the door.

"Get the hell out of this yard, you goddamn Nazis!" he yelled at them.

They left, looking over their shoulders at him, but still carrying on.

Shortly thereafter, Jelich came by the house. He was delivering copies of *Stars and Stripes,* the daily Army newspaper. Delivery of this paper was very erratic. When we were engaged in an action, nobody was bringing newspapers around, so we might go several days without seeing it. But today we were resting up and here it was. This was a treat.

Jelich gave me a copy and left. I offered to give Hillbilly a part of the paper, but he declined my offer to my immeasurable relief. I really didn't want to share the paper. I wanted it all for myself. Hillbilly was what educators call "a reluctant reader." I do not say that with any sense of superiority, for Hillbilly was not without knowledge. If I had stepped into his world and been tested in his strengths—farming, animal husbandry, and car repair—I would have scored as low as he did in reading, probably lower.

I looked for the Bill Mauldin cartoon. This was the best thing in the paper. I always turned to it first. But there was no cartoon today.

Next I always went to the war news from the Eastern front. I read this now slowly and carefully. I had been following the Russian advance closely, cheering them on. Every German they killed was one less that we had to kill.

I thought that Stalingrad was the key battle of the war. From then on, the Germans were in retreat and we knew they would lose the war.

I felt an immense debt of gratitude to the Russian Army. Think of the thousands upon thousands upon thousands of German soldiers they had killed. Think of the staggering number of German divisions they had destroyed. What if all those German soldiers and divisions had not been wiped off the board? What if they had been available to fight us on the Western front? It did not bear thinking about. We were having a tough-enough time with a weakened Germany. If there had been no Eastern front and the full power and might of the German Army had been arrayed against us on the Western front, how many more of us, including probably myself, would be dead? Every Russian who died was one less American who had to die.

On another page of *Stars and Stripes,* there was a story coming out of Paris. A bunch of guys in the Quartermaster Corps had been caught stealing. This was not a case of individual petty thievery. It was an organized ring. They had been stealing whole freight-car loads of cigarettes, worth millions of francs on the black market. They were court-martialed and given long prison sentences. Then the Army commuted the sentences and said that instead the men would be given six weeks of infantry training and then be sent to the front.

So now we knew what the Army really thought of us. We were considered a suitable dumping ground for criminals. Twenty years in prison or another fitting punishment, serve in a rifle company, take your pick. The Army was telling us what we already knew, that we were the lowest of the low, that we were fucked.

I never stole as much as a single cigarette and I was put in the infantry without a day's training. And who would want these guys in their outfit? A guy who was a big-time operator, who knew how to play the angles to his individual benefit, what kind of a soldier would he make? Would he dog it? Could you depend on him?

Then another story caught my eye. A group of G.I.'s were bogged down by a river. They crouched down, reluctant to leave the safety of the woods they were in.

A lone figure strode out of the mist and stood before them.

"Follow me, boys," he said and plunged into the river.

Emboldened by his action, the G.I.'s got up one by one and followed him. On the other side of the river, they quickly secured their objective and wanted to thank the man who had led them but he had disappeared.

"He never gave us his name," said one of the G.I.'s. "All I can say about him is this—he had three stars on his helmet and he was wearing two pearl-handled pistols."

Oh, for chrissakes. This was too much. He plunged into the river *in the wintertime?* They must think we're all a bunch of morons. The story no doubt had been planted by one of Patton's aides with either a gullible or cynical reporter. It was a preposterous fairy tale and yet I supposed years hence it would appear in a child's *Story of General Patton*. And, if you had a valuable general, why would you want to put him at risk by having him go anywhere near the front?

On the same page as Patton's walk-on-water story, there was an item about how a single American soldier had outwitted and tricked 50 Germans into surrendering by convincing them he had a whole battalion behind him. This sounded like something plagiarized from a Hollywood movie. These asshole reporters. I remembered one time our division was briefly mentioned in *Stars and Stripes.* In describing the movement of the division, the reporter wrote that the division had "darted." What were we, a chipmunk? It is impossible for a division to dart.

Sergeant Drummond came by. It was perfect timing. I had just set aside *Stars and Stripes.* I had read every single word in it and was ready to read more if only there had been more pages.

"Intelligence thinks the Krauts are getting information about us from somebody in this town," Sergeant Drummond said. "We think that somebody's got a radio and they're sending messages. So we're going to go out and search all the houses and look for the radio."

Sergeant Drummond, Hillbilly, and I went together. The first house we went to, the door was opened by a middle-aged man. His wife was standing apprehensively behind him. I told the man we had to look into every room but, of course, I didn't tell him what we were looking for.

He took us around.

The first door he opened was to a bedroom. There was a large bed in the center of the room. In the bed, under the covers, side by side, face up, lay a man and woman, his parents. They were dying together. They had wasted away. I doubted they each weighed eighty pounds. They were awake. Their eyes followed us. It was the only part of them that could move. Their skin was yellowish. Their eyes were sunken and with black around them.

They would never rise from this bed again. They would go from this bed into a wooden box. I was looking at the faces of imminent death. So this was what life held for those who lived the full cycle. We end up the same way we began, as helpless as babies.

We stood around the bed staring down at them. It seemed to me that we were trespassing on something terribly private.

There was nobody in the next house we went to. The people had fled. We checked the two floors. Then Sergeant Drummond said, "Hillbilly and me are going to check the cellar. Charley, you check the attic."

They went downstairs and I started up the stairs to the attic with some trepidation. What if the guy was waiting upstairs? What if he was prepared to go out in a hail of gunfire? Didn't they shoot spies? What did he have to lose?

I held my carbine at the ready, safety off. I had been relaxed with Sergeant Drummond and Hillbilly. But when you're alone, it's a different matter.

I went up the stairs slowly and quietly, listening hard.

The attic consisted of a room at the top of the stairs. I stood by the door, listening. I slowly turned the doorknob and then I kicked the door open and moved forward, ready to shoot.

It was a tiny room. There was nothing in it but a small table and one chair. On the table, very neatly folded, was a German soldier's uniform. It looked brand new. A deserter probably.

I told Sergeant Drummond what I had found.

"He's probably behind some horse in a field right now," Sergeant Drummond said.

We never did find the radio.

19

Commanders

AS I HAVE MENTIONED, I served under three battalion commanders, Colonel Rudd, Major Goode, and Major Pusey. Colonel Rudd,
a West Point graduate, was the scariest of the three. He could send
men to their death as calmly as if he were ordering a chicken sandwich in a restaurant. His mindset seemed to go something like this:
You're a soldier; you're expected to die; that's why you're here; so
don't make a big thing out of it. He would have made a stern judge;
I don't think the idea of mercy would have crossed his mind.

I overheard an officer make a very perceptive comment at the CP
one day when Colonel Rudd wasn't there. He said, "Rudd is the only
real soldier up here. The rest of us are civilians." What he meant was
that Rudd was a professional soldier and no one else was.

It wasn't that Rudd was cold and heartless, which implies a con-
scious rejection of human feeling. He didn't turn away from human
feeling. He didn't recognize it. He exhibited a steely self-control at all
times. He was like a man from another planet.

I did not "like" Colonel Rudd. Nobody "liked" him. He was a
force of nature. Liking or disliking him seemed irrelevant. I was more
afraid of him than anything else. He played no favorites. He was fair.
He treated everybody the same, but he was a stern taskmaster, espe-

cially with the other officers. I think they were glad when he was wounded and evacuated. Now they could relax a little.

A prolonged artillery attack makes you hypersensitive to sound. A driver started up his 2 1/2 ton truck and we all hit the ground, except Colonel Rudd, who remained standing. We all laughed as we got up, feeling foolish. He made no comment. Little jokes were beyond him. In fact, he hadn't seemed to notice us lying on the ground.

But there was, undeniably, a chilling quality about him. I thought of that one night after he left and I was alone with the new commander, Major Goode, at battalion CP. It was in the middle of the night, about two in the morning.

One of our rifle companies was in a defensive position along a known, fixed line. The Germans laid down intense mortar fire and then their infantry attacked. The American lieutenant in command was killed and his radio operator badly wounded. There were no noncoms in their vicinity to take over so a private grabbed the radio and managed to call battalion CP. He pleaded with me for artillery fire. I turned him over to Major Goode.

The private, a rifleman, didn't know normal radio procedure. He just talked so Major Goode did the same thing.

"We need artillery here! The Krauts are all around us!"

"Are they close?"

"They're on top of us!"

"I can't call in artillery! They can't cut it that fine! Some of the rounds will land on you!"

"We have to risk it, sir! They're going to overrun us!"

"I can't do that to you!"

"You've got to call it in, sir! It's our only chance!"

Major Goode called it in and then he returned to the private.

"What's your name, son?"

He told him.

"I just want to tell you how brave you are and how much I admire you for it."

The artillery started. The private was going to report back on the effectiveness of the rounds.

Major Goode turned and looked directly into my eyes. His eyes were wet and shiny. He wanted to make human contact with me, with somebody.

"Those poor fellows are dying out there," he said to me.

The distress was evident in his face and voice.

Major Goode agonized over those riflemen. Colonel Rudd would not have agonized. He would not have engaged the private in personal conversation. He would not have asked his name and he would not have told him he admired his bravery. He would not have said to him, as Major Goode did, "I hope you make it out of this." He would not have spoken to me. He would not have looked at me. I didn't count.

Major Goode was more human than Colonel Rudd, but was he a better commander than Rudd? No, he was not. He had the fatal flaw of indecisiveness, perhaps the result of too much humanity, and he made everyone uneasy. In a perilous situation, everyone knew that Rudd would not shrink from what needed to be done. Maybe compassion makes difficult decisions even more difficult.

When Rudd met with the officers of the rifle companies to go over the plan of operations, he was in command. He spoke and they listened. When Goode met with the officers, it was more democratic. He allowed the officers to speak. He began some sentences with three un-Rudd-like words, "Do you think . . . ?" It wasn't exactly a town-hall meeting but it was unsettling. You sensed that the officers had less confidence in him than they had had in Rudd. Maybe because he had less confidence in himself than Rudd had had in himself.

I personally liked Goode a lot. He yelled at me once in the stress of the situation. I was trying desperately to hear a transmission.

"I can't hear him, sir," I said.

"Goddamn it, soldier, what the hell's the matter with you?" he shouted.

He grabbed the receiver off me and held it to his ear and didn't have any better luck.

"I'm sorry—it wasn't your fault," he said.

He had apologized to me, amazingly, in front of other officers, the first and last apology I ever received from an officer.

Each commander was different. They even slept differently. During an engagement, Colonel Rudd didn't sleep. He remained seated at the table all night long in battalion CP. He was in charge of everything, night and day.

Major Goode couldn't sleep. He worried. He would lie down in his blankets in a darkened corner of the room but he was awake. I would suddenly hear him.

"Has he called back yet?"

"No, sir. He hasn't."

"If he calls, be sure to wake me."

"Yes, sir. I will."

But I never had to wake him.

The CP could be absolutely quiet for an hour at three in the morning. If I got a call, the minute he heard my voice, he would pop up on the floor, sit up.

"What is it?"

On the other hand, Major Pusey, Major Goode's successor, would lie down on his cot and sleep like a baby. I think that was because at his core, ambition aside, he was indifferent to what happened.

I liked being Major Pusey's operator. I knew that with him I was going to be as safe as I ever was going to be. I had dreaded going out with Colonel Rudd, who was adventurous and foolhardy. There was no telling where he might go. And, as his radio operator, I had to tag along with him wherever he went. The words I never wanted to hear again were, "Let's go see what's going on." He wanted to be close to the action. He was always leaving five or six officers back at the CP and setting up an OP (Observation Post) with just him and me. He just didn't care about his own ass.

Now Major Pusey did care about his own ass. And since I cared about my ass, he and I had something very important in common. Major Pusey was not adventurous and foolhardy. He didn't want to be close to the action. He never set up an OP in his life. That was why, even though I detested the man, I much preferred going out with Major Pusey to going out with Colonel Rudd. The best single word I would use to describe Pusey is: *prudent*.

He was even prudent with me. If an enemy observer sees two soldiers moving together, one of whom has a radio strapped to his back, he will make the assumption that the other soldier is an officer and officers are prime targets. There were times when I made Major Pusey nervous by my proximity to him.

"Don't stand near me!" he said sharply to me once.

Another time he barked at me, "Get away from me!" as if I had a contagious disease.

Colonel Rudd never told me to get away from him. He didn't seem to be aware that I was making him the bull's eye.

But Major Pusey's prudence almost cost me my life once. The battalion's objective was to take a particular town. One of our rifle companies went in and succeeded in taking the lower end of the town but then they were stopped cold in their tracks. Every time a rifleman showed his face in the street, he was greeted by an 88 shell that came down with pinpoint accuracy. The Germans obviously had eyes somewhere. Nobody dared venture out into the street. The riflemen hid behind houses and pondered what to do next.

It was at this point, a stalemate, with the Germans occupying the upper end of town and the Americans occupying the lower end, that Major Pusey and I made our way toward the town.

Several battalion staff officers had gone on ahead into town and set up a CP in a house furthest from the Germans. The house was just beyond an open field. To get to the CP, Major Pusey and I had to cross this field.

There were some bushes at the edge of the field. We crouched low behind these bushes and looked the situation over. It was a long field, appeared to be close to a hundred yards in length. That was a long way to go. And it was believed that this field was under enemy observation. There was a deep ditch that traversed the length of the field. Clearly it would be smart to run next to the ditch.

"I'm going to go first," Major Pusey said. "You wait here. The CP is that blue house on the right. When you see me get to it, then you can start across."

I thought that was a good idea. Two soldiers together make a more inviting target than one soldier alone. Of course, I knew that Pusey didn't want to be anywhere near my radio.

Major Pusey then jumped up and started across. I peered through the bushes and watched him anxiously. He was running but he was a big man and carried a lot of weight. I watched him huffing and puffing. I figured I could get across in half the time it took him. He was a quarter of the way. Halfway. Three-quarters. He was out of the field and into the house. Whew! Nothing had happened. That was a very good sign. Maybe the field was not under observation.

I took several deep breaths because I was going to run this at top speed and I wanted to prepare my lungs.

I jumped up and started across. I hadn't taken five steps into the field when I heard the approaching whistle of an 88 coming straight for my head. I had been running alongside the ditch. I dove into it.

There were five inches of ice water running along the bottom of the ditch. I lay, face down, stretched out in this water. After the explosion, the first words out of my mouth were, "That goddamn son-of-a-bitch Pusey!"

They had been waiting for me. They hadn't been ready for him but his crossing had alerted them so that when I started, they were ready for me. He had set me up for this by crossing alone. If I had crossed with Colonel Rudd, he would have said, "Let's go!" and we would have crossed together because that was how he did things and I would now be sitting safely at the CP. We would have had the element of surprise on our side. Instead I was lying in some ice water with about ninety yards ahead of me. That bastard Pusey.

I was very grateful for the ditch. It had clearly saved my life. Of course, if the shell had landed in the ditch, it would have been a different story.

The ice water was working its way through my clothes. The ice water was the rent money I had to pay for the use of the ditch. I would gladly pay it any day of the week because you can always dry your clothes off but you can't get undead, not even once.

I waited several minutes to see if there were any follow-up rounds. Nothing came. I jumped out of the ditch, heart pounding, sprinted like Jesse Owens, made maybe twenty yards, another one came, dove into the ditch, got up, ran thirty yards, another one, dove in again, got up, ran, nothing more came. I guess they gave up. Three shells. All close.

The stalemate was finally broken. Some rifleman with sharp eyes detected movement inside the top of the church steeple. It was a German hiding in the belfry. The church was the tallest building in town and the belfry provided a great view of everything. That observer was their eyes. Anything that moved was fired upon. When he saw a target, he would radio down to a Tiger Royal that was hiding behind a barn. The Tiger Royal would pop out, fire an 88, and then hide again.

A fire mission was called in to the artillery and they blew the upper half of the church to smithereens. Spumoni got terribly upset when he heard about it.

"We shouldn't have done that," he said. "It's not right. We should leave the church out of it."

Poor Spumoni. He was a real idealist, true to his hallucination of heaven even at the risk of his own life, in contrast to those paper idealists who play with concepts.

A couple of years later I was describing what it was like to go out with the battalion commander, and my brother said to me, "Did you ever stop to think that maybe the officer wasn't the target? Maybe you were the target because of the importance of your radio."

That really shook me up. I had always assumed the officer was the target. Could this be true? That I was the target or, more accurately, that my radio was the target? Which theory is true? I have no idea.

But if the alternative theory is correct, then that day in crossing the field, it wouldn't have mattered if I crossed with Pusey or alone, since I was the target. But I don't believe my radio had anything to do with it. That first shell came the moment I entered the field. They didn't have time to spot my radio, calculate my distance, send the message, and fire. I remain convinced that Pusey's crossing had alerted them and they were waiting for me. A small matter, no doubt, and of no interest to anyone but myself, but I like to try and understand what really happened.

Of course, Major Pusey could not have known his crossing first was going to put me in jeopardy, so it was irrational of me to curse him. But when your life is threatened, it's hard to be rational.

20

Folenius

THE ARMY WANTED TO boost the morale of its front-line infantrymen. The news came down to us. One enlisted man from each battalion would be sent to Paris on a three-day pass. Actually, it was a seven-day pass, with four days spent in travel and three days in Paris. To be fair about it, the lucky infantryman would not be selected by anyone. A lottery would be held. A box filled with folded slips of paper would be brought around. Each infantryman without looking would stick his arm in the box and pull out one slip of paper. Most likely, he would pull out a blank slip. But there was one slip in there with the winning word on it. What was the winning word? Nobody knew. Was it *Hallelujah!?* Was it *Paris?* Was it *Whores?* Was it two words, *Parisian Whores?*

When I heard about the lottery, I felt in fairness the drawing should be restricted to the men in the rifle companies. They were the ones who really had it rough. They were the ones in the most danger. They were the ones who deserved the pass the most. I did not feel support personnel on the battalion level should be eligible. Of course, that would mean communications people would be excluded from the drawing. But should the battalion mail clerk be the one to go to Paris? When there was heavy fighting going on, he would disappear and show up three days later when things had quieted down with our mail and act like it had taken him three days to go to the rear and get it.

I expressed my sentiments to Sergeant Drummond, not mentioning any specific job categories that should be ineligible, but just saying I thought the drawing should be restricted to the riflemen because they deserved it the most.

"I think you'll have a hard time convincing the fellows of that," Sergeant Drummond said dryly. "Of course, if you feel that strongly about it, when it's your turn to draw, just pass."

I didn't feel that strongly about it. I drew but came up with a blank slip. And wouldn't you know it? The lucky guy turned out to be Kenny Groton, a battalion radio operator. What was the winning word? I have forgotten.

Groton got in the back of a 2 1/2 ton truck, along with the winners from other battalions, and off they went. Groton spent three days in Paris, drinking and screwing, eating little, sleeping little. When he climbed back in the 2 1/2 ton truck for the return trip, he was worn out. He curled up on the bed of the truck and slept most of the way across France. When he pulled in to where we were staying, he noticed a wet feeling in his underpants. He pulled down his pants and investigated. A thick, yellow pus was oozing out of his dick. He had the clap. He got off the truck and got into an ambulance for a trip to a hospital in the rear for treatment. We didn't even see him till much later.

So much for the widely held belief among the G.I.'s that the whores of Paris were "clean," that is, free of disease.

The Army wanted to improve morale, and who can fault them for that? But the misadventure of one of our own backed up on the battalion radio operators. We had always been stretched thin but now with the absence of the gonorrheal Groton, we were severely short-handed. It would have been nice if Sergeant Drummond had voluntarily grabbed a radio and helped out, but he wasn't about to do that. He didn't want to set a precedent.

We were quartered in a town that was close to a dark and forbidding forest. The order was given to advance into the forest. We set up the battalion CP a short distance inside the woods. Our CP was an abandoned German CP, built by them when they had the time and the will to do the job right. It was an underground bunker. The door to it opened on the German side. Well-built, wooden stairs sloped down to the door. You walked down the stairs and entered a good-sized room. There was a long table going the length of the room, east to west. There were more than enough chairs at the table. To the left of the table alongside the wall was a row of four double bunks, eight beds, wooden, very sturdy The ceiling was massive; huge timbers spanned the width of the room. On top of this ceiling or roof was a good six feet of earth. While we were there, several 88s scored direct hits on this earth cover above us. The ground shook and we looked up but no one was inclined to dive for the wooden floor. We felt a comfortable separation from the power of the shell. It was the safest CP I had ever been in. I was deeply appreciative of the marvelous building skills of the Germans, their engineering talent and their careful workmanship. It was such an impressive room I felt the Germans had not built it for a unit so lowly as a battalion. It must have been designed a CP for at least the regiment or division level.

There was a small clearing alongside the CP. In midafternoon of the first day, two cooks came to serve us a hot meal. They were in a jeep pulling a trailer. They parked in the clearing. They took three big pots of hot food plus an urn of hot coffee from the trailer and set them on the hood of the jeep and began serving. First to be fed were the officers in the CP. Next were the riflemen. They were close by, positioned behind trees. Two or three of them drifted back at a time, mess gear in hand. The idea was to have no more than five or six guys clustered together. I got in line with the riflemen. I looked on anxiously as each man got his kit filled to overflowing. I was really looking forward to this meal and no matter how much food there is before you in pots, you don't really believe you will get your share until it is safely in your own mess kit. A dog knows the feeling.

And then I was served. I turned away from the jeep, very pleased indeed, intending to eat in the CP. Suddenly I heard the whistling of an 88. It landed short, in our general vicinity, close enough to make us flinch, but not close enough to make us hit the ground. In a panic the cooks grabbed the pots and the urn and hurriedly set them back in the trailer. They jumped in the jeep and just before they sped away, the trailer bouncing up and down, the cook on the passenger side called out to me, "We'd stay but we can't risk losing the vehicle!"

Wow! What luck! I was the last guy to get fed. And the cooks' sudden departure left a lot of riflemen who were going to go hungry. They would have to make do with the maddening aroma in their nostrils from the laden mess gear of their more fortunate buddies. It is a fact that the continued experienced of being hungry sharpens the sense of smell until one begins to develop the olfactory powers of man's best friend.

We never saw the cooks again in those woods. But what well-trained soldiers they were. Their nurturing instincts were to feed those riflemen but their training gave them the necessary discipline to set that aside. Their primary concern had to be the safety of that jeep. They truly understood the import of the training film we all saw—"Take care of your equipment and your equipment will take care of you."

That night I felt the urgent call of nature, to do No. 2. I went outside and I didn't want to do it too close to the CP where we might step in it so I walked a few yards into the forest. I unbuckled my pants and squatted but before I did anything, a shell came hurtling out of the sky. I threw myself forward and flattened against the ground. The thought crossed my mind: Wouldn't this be something if I got killed because I had to take a crap? The pattern was, if one shell came, two or three more followed. So after the first one, I jumped up and raced for the bunker, holding my pants up with one hand, not taking the time to button then.

In the pitch-black darkness, I ran headlong into a tree. It was like someone had socked me in the jaw. It knocked me flat on my ass. I was lucky that my glasses weren't damaged. Somewhat dazed, I got up and continued my flight back to the bunker but at a more judicious pace.

Afterwards, I realized I had probably precipitated the shelling. When I opened the door to go out, the light from the lamps inside flashed in the dark forest. The flash could have been seen. And after all, the Germans built the CP. They knew where it was located with pinpoint preciseness.

I sat at that table in the CP with the receiver pressed to my ear the first day and the first night and the second day and the second night and the third morning. The officers could take naps in the bunks and did but I could not. By twelve noon of the third day, I had been on duty for fifty-two straight hours. It was the longest period of time I had ever gone without sleeping. I was groggy from not eating but I did not have to fight off sleep. I had not even come close to nodding off. I was suspended in some strange state of consciousness.

At one o'clock in the afternoon of the third day, Jelich arrived at the CP with a jeepload of people. He brought with him Folenius, a radio operator and my relief. He also had with him Sergeant Henderson, the ranking noncom in communications. Sergeant Drummond handled the radio duties but Sergeant Henderson outranked him. He was in overall charge of both wire and radio.

The third fellow who came along in the jeep was the New Guy. He was a fresh replacement and our new apprentice radio operator. This was his first day on the job, so to speak. Sergeant Drummond was busy. He had gone back to Regiment to get a couple of new radio batteries. So Sergeant Henderson had brought the New Guy along so that he could sit at the table and observe Folenius at work. Folenius would break him in. Everybody referred to him as the New Guy because there had been no time to get acquainted. I don't know if anybody knew his name. He was good-looking, black-haired, slender, medium height. He seemed like a nice guy, quiet.

I turned my radio over to Folenius and left with Jelich. He would drive me back to town. Then he would come back to the CP for Sergeant Henderson. By that time Henderson should be ready to leave.

As we came into town, Jelich asked me, "You hungry? You want me to stop by the kitchen?"

I was too tired to eat.

"No. I just want to sleep."

I had discovered that in the competition between exhaustion and hunger, exhaustion wins.

Jelich dropped me off at our house. Nobody was there. I quickly spread out my blankets, sat down on them, took off my helmet, hurriedly unlaced my boots and tore them off. It was a race to see if I could get them off before I fell asleep. I left all my clothes on and fell asleep in the very act of lying down.

I slept for about a minute and then I began to dream. A voice way off in the distance was calling my name. How the hell did they know I was here? I didn't have the energy to respond. I just ignored it. No matter how many times they called, I wasn't going to answer. I knew I could outlast them. As long as I could keep on sleeping, I didn't care what they did.

Then somebody shook me.

I pretended not to notice. What the hell was going on here? This was starting to get annoying.

Somebody shook me again, harder.

Goddamn it!

I rolled over, to get away from it.

"Charley, wake up!"

Was I hearing things?

"Charley, wake up!"

"Wha-wha-wha-wha-wha?"

"Wake up!"

I opened my eyes. I blinked. It was Sergeant Drummond.

"You've got to go back to the CP and take over," he said.

This was too much. I was going to go crazy if I couldn't sleep.

"Jesus Christ!" I said angrily. "Am I the only radio operator in this outfit?"

Sergeant Drummond was looking at me somberly.

"Henderson and Folenius are dead," he said.

"Oh, my God," I breathed.

"And the New Guy was wounded. That's why we need you."

I sat up and reached for a boot.

I wasn't sleepy anymore. I felt sick at the news.

"What happened?"

"An 88 came down the stairs and blew the door off. They were sitting by the door."

The stairs! I hadn't thought of the stairs! A shell from the American side couldn't have entered the bunker. The trajectory was wrong. But a shell from the German side apparently could and did.

We drove back in silence. When we got to the CP, the dead and wounded had already been removed. None of the officers were hurt. It seemed that the shell did not enter the CP. If it had, some of the officers would surely have been killed. But apparently it exploded outside the bunker, on the stairs, but close enough to the door to do the damage.

The officers were like zombies. They didn't talk to one another. They didn't look at each other. They just sat there, stupefied. I had never seen a CP that quiet. Each man was in his own world.

Jelich wasn't there now but he had been there. Later when we were alone, he told me what happened. Sergeant Henderson, the New Guy, and Folenius had been sitting together at the table at the end closest to the door. Jelich had been sitting next to Sergeant Henderson, waiting for him to decide when to leave. Henderson was giving the New Guy instructions. Moments before the shell hit, Captain Bacovitch called Jelich over to the other end of the table, the officers' side of the room. He wanted to ask Jelich a question. Jelich had been standing by Captain Bacovitch's chair when the shell exploded.

It was very difficult for Jelich to talk about it.

"Folenius died right away," he said. "Henderson lived three or four minutes. He was looking at me. Blood was bubbling out of his throat. 'Help me, help me,' he kept saying." Jelich shook his head. "But what could I do?"

It was as if I were there. I could see the look in Henderson's eyes. He knew he was dying and he didn't want to die. He didn't want to leave what he had back home. He was deeply in love with his wife.

They bound up the New Guy's wounds as best they could and rushed him to battalion aid in Jelich's jeep.

"Doc says he's going to be all right," Jelich said, "but he's going to lose a leg."

Six months before, the New Guy had been a civilian. He lived in Los Angeles with his mother. His first day in combat was his last. He would go home minus a leg but at least he would go home.

We called Sergeant Henderson the Sock Man because he used to come around with his sock bag about once a week to collect our dirty socks. Later he would give us clean ones. Socks were the only article of clothing the Army was concerned about.

He was a genuinely nice man, always genial, always good-natured. His face was open and trusting, definitely not a big-city kind of face. He wore his authority lightly. I liked him a lot. He was only in his late twenties but he was already losing his hair. His hairline was retreating.

The noteworthy fact about Sergeant Henderson was that he loved his wife so much. He was the only guy in communications who was married. His face softened when he spoke of her. He got that far-away look.

One night when the guys were joking around, talking about girls, one of the very few times we talked about girls, Sergeant Henderson sat there listening. Then he said quietly, shaking his head, "You guys don't know what it's like to be married. You have no idea."

He told me privately one day that he wanted to take his wife to Tahiti.

"I keep having this same dream," he said. "She and I are living together on a magic island, away from civilization. I know it's a crazy dream. You can't live that way. But I keep having the dream."

He had been married four weeks when the Army shipped him to Iceland. That was three years ago. He hadn't seen her since.

I always thought that the war was a lot harder on him than it was on me. Every day apart from her was torture for him. He so desperately wanted to be with her that when he had the free time to think about it, he was in torment. I had nobody so I didn't have that additional pain. I had my family, of course, but a family is not the same thing as a wife or sweetheart.

Harry Folenius was from Hamilton, Ohio. He was boyish, curly-haired. He had a face that belonged on one of those little kids in an *Our Gang* movie. I could see girls looking at his picture and crying, "Oh, he's so cute!" He was a good guy, easy to get along with. Everybody liked him.

His proudest possession was an air mattress to sleep on because he knew he was the only guy who had one. Every night, when we were in a house, he would pump it up with a bicycle pump and then in the morning deflate it and roll it up. I wondered where he got it.

It was a narrow mattress, just wide enough for one person. It made strange sounds when he moved on it.

I knew very little about Folenius. What did he do in civilian life? I had no idea. As a matter of fact, I didn't know what any of the fellows did in civilian life. Nobody talked about the past. It just wasn't done. I didn't tell anyone I had been to college. This was contrary to war movies wherein the soldiers recite their personal history at the drop of a hat. They do so freely, without any encouragement, with no self-consciousness. But I could see where our reticence might be a good thing. If you knew your sergeant had held some lowly job before he was drafted, it could affect your attitude toward him. It might undermine his authority. This way we were all equal. You weren't judged on your former position in society. You were judged by what you did in the here and now.

At the same time I wish I could have learned more about the background of each man in my outfit. But once in a while, someone opened the curtain a little bit. That happened to Folenius and me one night when we were alone in a house, lying down, getting ready to go to sleep. I don't know what prompted him to speak. I guess he was just feeling mellow. It was not a dialogue. It was a monologue. He didn't expect or want a response from me. He just wanted to get something off his chest. The subject was his older sister.

He spoke of her with great, reminiscent feeling. Apparently she had taken care of him when he was growing up. She looked after him. He spoke of all the things she had done for him. It was apparent that he loved her very much. I got the distinct impression that she was a surrogate mother to him. And he never mentioned his parents. So I started thinking: Did he have any parents? Was he an orphan and his sister had taken over the responsibility of raising him? Or had his parents kicked him out and she took him into her own home? But, of course, I didn't dare ask. And I really didn't know. It was all conjecture on my part. But that he was bonded to his sister out of love and gratitude, that was not conjecture.

After Folenius's death, I inherited his .45. Sergeant Drummond brought it to me a couple of days later, along with its holster and two clips of bullets. There was a dark stain on the holster that I was sure was blood. This was the prized weapon because all the officers carried one. I felt special with it on my hip. And it had a great benefit for me. It left both my arms free when I carried my radio on my back. I didn't have to fool around with the carbine, which I slung on my shoulder and which kept slipping off if I didn't hold it on with one hand. So I gladly gave up a perfectly good weapon, my carbine, for a weapon that was practically useless because of its very limited range. A pistol was like a bayonet. By the time you got close enough to use it, you'd be dead.

Along with his .45, I inherited Folenius's rank. He was a T/5, technician fifth grade, the equivalent of a corporal, two stripes. I was now promoted to T/5 with a commensurate increase in pay from $50 a month to $66.

When I was being drafted, my grandfather said to the family in front of me, "With his education, he'll be a sergeant in two weeks."

It was his way of diminishing in advance any possible success on my part. If I had made sergeant in two weeks, he would have said, "It's to be expected. After all, he went to college. With an advantage like that, it doesn't surprise me."

But I didn't make sergeant in two weeks. Instead I remained a private for almost two full years. I didn't even make PFC, private first class, at $54 a month. I can imagine what my grandfather said about that.

But now I had some rank. I didn't have to put "Pvt." in front of my name when I wrote home. I could put "T/5." I didn't have to feel like such a failure.

Chance dictates everything.

One afternoon Jelich was driving me forward in his jeep. Another jeep passed us going in the opposite direction, to the rear. On the hood of the jeep sat two German prisoners. They were talking excitedly and laughing, joyful to be out of it. They felt safe. Their jeep took a direct hit from an 88, killing the two prisoners and the driver.

And so it was with Harry Folenius. He was sitting in my chair when he was killed. When he came into the bunker to relieve me, I stood up from my chair and he sat down in it and took over my radio. I sat in that chair for fifty-three straight hours and nothing happened to me. He sat in it for less than one hour and was killed. Chance dictates everything. Who was that jackanapes who said, "I am the master of my fate"?

What if Folenius had arrived at the bunker one hour later? The thought gives one pause. It could easily have happened. Folenius had to wait for Jelich and Henderson to pick him up, and the two first had to go to an adjoining town to pick up the New Guy. Jelich and Henderson could easily have been delayed an hour. They might have had trouble finding the New Guy. He might not have been where he was supposed to be. They might have run a last-minute errand for one of the cooks or the Supply Sergeant or an officer, an extra side trip. They might have stopped at the kitchen to eat a hot meal and relax for a bit. But they were not delayed. They delivered Folenius to the bunker just in time to get killed.

I do not feel guilty about Folenius's death. I did nothing to feel guilty about. He had to take his chances like we all did. But I can't help but feel that he died in my place.

He was 23 years old. "Have a little respect. I'm older than you are," he joked with me. Not anymore. I became 30, 40, 50, 60, 70. He remained 23. He will always be 23. I have grandsons older than that.

He was deprived of life, of loving someone, of holding his child in his arms, of lying in bed Sunday morning reading the paper, of watching a movie, of smelling freshly baked bread, of tasting a ripe nectarine, of walking down a quiet country lane, of all the thousand-and-one pleasures of life. If he could talk, would he say to me, "I died. You lived. Why?" And I have no answer to that.

One day my little daughter was on the grass in the yard, sitting on a bright blue plastic air mattress. She was pretending the mattress was a boat and she was out on the ocean, riding the waves. As I looked at her boat, it turned into a shabby brown air mattress and I saw Folenius sinking down into it and saying, "Ah, this is really living!"

All these years I have been haunted by a ghost. He is boyish, curly-haired. It is the ghost of Harry Folenius. As I wander through the banquet of life, he is always at my side. He never speaks. He just looks on. And as I get older, I am more and more aware of his presence.

21

Frankfurt

IT WAS MARCH 27, 1945. The city of Frankfurt-am-Main was our objective. To get into the city, we had to cross a bridge over the River Main. The Germans knew we had to cross here so there was no mystery as to where their artillery would be aimed. It would be aimed at the bridge.

The rifle companies crossed, followed by some of the battalion staff officers who proceeded to set up a CP in an apartment building. It was then that I was summoned. They needed a radio operator. So I set out alone to find the CP with my trusty radio on my back.

I was told by Sergeant Drummond about the bridge. "It's under observation. It's been getting heavy fire. Just run across it as fast as you can."

I stood behind a building and peeked around the corner at the bridge. It was a long way across, longer than I wanted it to be. And before you got on it, you had to be out in the open for a short distance. It was a stone bridge, built to last. Despite all the shell fire it had taken, it still looked pretty darn substantial. It was littered with debris, big piles of stuff, wrecked vehicles, mounds of every conceivable kind of junk. In places it looked like there was just enough room for me to get by.

I wasn't looking forward to this. For one thing I wasn't feeling well. Anything physical was an effort to do. I knew I wasn't my usual speedy self. The longer I was on the bridge, the worse for me. I would just have to do the best I could.

(There's a moment for you—the moment before you start off. It's like throwing down the dice with all your money on the table. Except it's not your money on the table, it's your life.)

An 88 would hit the bridge. I had to assume that. The question was, Where on the bridge would it hit and where on the bridge would I be when it hit? If the two places coincided, that would not be good.

This was Russian roulette, a matter of pure luck. Was I drawing one of my last breaths on this earth? I uttered a prayer. *O Lord, please get me through this one more time.*

Well, here goes.

I took a deep breath and with pounding heart took off.

It wasn't long in coming. Three of them, almost simultaneously. I threw myself down and tried to burrow sideways into the junk, trying to use it as a shield. With the explosions still ringing in my ears, I jumped up and started off again. I ran in some kind of suspended state and with mounting disbelief. Nothing was coming. I made it off the bridge and got behind a building. I was gasping for air.

I forgot to thank the Lord.

I screamed in silent exultation, mouthing the words, "I'm still here, you cocksuckers! You haven't done me in yet!"

After I calmed down, I proceeded up the street. I had to find the CP. I just had a general idea of where it was, and there was no cop on the corner to ask directions of. The street was deserted. It was a wide street. I was in a shopping district. There were stores on both sides of the street. I surmised this was one of the better shopping districts. The stores looked spacious and prosperous.

All the store windows had been shattered by shell fire. All the window displays were empty. I soon found out why. Looters. One came down the street toward me. He was pushing a cart, one of those big farm carts with a bar in the front. He was behind the bar, bent forward, pushing it. The cart was loaded to overflowing with all kinds of goods, but mostly clothing. And then lo and behold, there came another cart, going up the street like I was, but this one was empty. The guy was late to the party. The two carts met in the middle of the street. The two men exchanged heated words. And then the man with the empty cart grabbed some goods from the full cart and started throwing them in his cart. The looter with the ample inventory cried out in outrage and tried to repossess his goods. The two of them each had hold of a coat and were engaged in a tug of war, all the while screaming at each other. Just then shells started landing on the street. I had been hugging the line of doorways. I now dove into a doorway and flattened myself. To my amazement I saw that the two men didn't pay any attention to the falling shells. They continued their quarrel although death could come at any moment. They continued to stand upright in the middle of the street and tussle over the goods and scream imprecations at each other.

What was one to make of people?

I continued on my way.

I came to a block of what had been big apartment houses. They had been flattened by our Air Corps and a long time ago. Grass was growing out of cracks in the rubble.

Then a big, meaty man came walking toward me. I observed him closely. He was clean and well dressed, maybe forty-five years old. I was struck by his posture, his rigid backbone. I thought, No one walks like that unless he is a military man. He was wearing civilian clothes but that didn't mean anything. I kept my eyes on him.

He came up to me.

"Have you a Chesterfield?" he said in perfect English. He wasn't intimidated by me in the slightest.

I looked at him coldly and shook my head. I wouldn't have given him one if I had any. I didn't like his looks. He looked like a Nazi to me. He had small pig eyes and they were coldly measuring me. I thought, I don't know what you've done, but you're not clean, you son of a bitch. And what was he doing, wandering around the streets, with the fighting still going on?

The CP was supposed to be around here somewhere. Five blocks from the bridge, Sergeant Drummond said, and I had gone five blocks.

Two riflemen were guarding a group of about twenty prisoners who were up against an apartment building. The prisoners all had their hands on top of their heads. They were young kids, maybe four-teen, fifteen years old, some with rosy cheeks. If Hitler was down to using kids, that was a good sign.

I asked one of the riflemen if he knew where the CP was and he made a gesture of around the corner. I found it. On the first floor of an apartment building. Only one officer was in there, Captain Ba-covitch. I sat down at the table and got my radio going.

Lieutenant Tidwell came in.

"A bunch of firemen just surrendered to O'Neill," he said. "They were all old guys. They were given rifles two days ago."

Major Pusey arrived about thirty minutes later. He got on the radio and told Brierly, his driver, to bring the jeep across. I thought that was kind of risky. There was too much debris on the bridge.

Some time after that, Brierly walked in.

"You get through all right?" Major Pusey said to him.

"I had to leave the jeep on the bridge," Brierly said.

"You *what?*" Major Pusey exploded. His eyes were big with anger. "You go back there and get that jeep! Don't come back here without it!"

Sure enough, the debris had slowed Brierly down. Then the shells came. He jumped out of the jeep and ran for his life.

White-faced, Brierly reluctantly left the CP and returned to the bridge. Well, at least now we knew which was more valuable, a man's life or a vehicle.

But I had to give Brierly credit. He did bring the jeep back. It had been wounded, with holes in its windshield and various pieces of shrapnel buried in the seats, but it was still running.

22

Finis

BY EARLY APRIL it had become clear to me that something very alarming was going on inside my body. I was feeling awful. I had constant, racking headaches. I lost my appetite completely. I had to force myself to eat and I would only pick at the food. I felt terribly weak, with no energy, no strength. I was dragging myself around. It was bad enough just sitting and handling radio messages, but if physical exertion was required, if I had to walk any distance with the radio on my back, it took every ounce of strength I had to make it. Something was happening to me and I had no idea what it was. I only knew I had never felt this bad in my life. Last year in the States I had had tonsillitis, with raging fever, burning up, but this was different. No fever. Just a general collapse of my body.

Every day I felt worse, and this had been going on for two weeks.

One day I sat slumped on some stairs with my mess gear on my lap. I couldn't eat the food. An old German woman chanced by.

"*Krank,*" she said, nodding sympathetically. "*Krank.*"

I didn't have the energy to reply.

"You look terrible," Jelich said to me.

"I feel terrible," I said.

"Why don't you go see the doc?" he suggested.

I was reluctant to do so. What could I tell him? That I felt lousy? He'd boot my ass out of there fast if that was all I could tell him. What I needed was a visible sign that he could look at and I didn't have one.

And then I got one. I was standing and urinating one afternoon when I noticed my flow was red. I rejoiced. At last I had a sign that he could see.

I went to battalion aid the next morning.

The last time I had gone to Captain Sawyer was about a month back. I had had the runs real bad. He gave me a shot of paregoric for it, which I enjoyed drinking. It tasted like a shot of whiskey. It did the trick.

I waited patiently for Captain Sawyer to turn his attention to me. Finally he did so. He looked at me with a face of wary skepticism. I suppose that was only natural, for he was the one guy who could punch your ticket out of here and I am sure he had learned to be distrustful of most stories.

"Sir," I said, "I've been feeling real lousy for the last two weeks. I have these sick headaches and I can't eat. I've lost my appetite."

He interrupted my litany.

"Do you throw up?"

"No, sir. I don't. But I have this terrible fatigue. I can hardly move. I feel weak." Then I gave him the punch line. "And yesterday I noticed I was urinating red, a deep red."

Captain Sawyer grunted. He didn't seem too impressed. He turned to a medic and said something. Then he walked away. The medic went to a box of medicines and started rummaging around in there. He took out a little white envelope. He handed me the envelope.

"Take one of these with a little water every time you feel a headache coming on. If one doesn't do any good, then take two."

I looked in the envelope. There were about a dozen little white pills.

"What are these?" I asked.

"Aspirins."

I nodded.

"Okay, thanks."

I left.

I took the aspirins. They didn't do any good whatsoever.

I was thinking, Why is it that I know I'm sick and Jelich knows I'm sick and that German woman knows I'm sick, and the goddamn doctor doesn't know I'm sick? What the hell is wrong with him? Isn't pissing red a sign of something?

A couple of days later I saw Jelich looking at me funny.

"Jesus, Charley, your eyeballs are yellow," he said.

"They are?" I said.

"I'll say. And your skin is yellow, too. You're changing into a Chinaman."

I went back to Captain Sawyer. I was moderately pissed off. I didn't repeat any of my symptoms, not even pissing red, which I was still doing.

"Sir, guys have been telling me my eyeballs are yellow."

I increased Jelich to plural observers because I felt that would be more effective in getting his attention.

He took his blunt fingers and put them on my cheekbone and pulled down hard on the skin, opening my eye wide. He peered at it.

"Oh!" he said brightly. "You've got yellow jaundice!"

Hallelujah! I had something! My sickness had been acknowledged! I wasn't alone with it anymore. I felt an enormous sense of relief.

Captain Sawyer spoke to a medic. The medic came over to me and said, "Give me your helmet and cartridge belt."

I did so.

He put them on a table.

There was a stretcher on the floor by the wall. The medic indicated the stretcher.

"Lie down on this stretcher," he said.

I obeyed with alacrity. I had been feeling dizzy and it felt mighty good to get off my feet.

Lie down on this stretcher. What a lovely command, so full of possibilities, so rich in promise. Things were looking up.

The medic came over and draped a blanket over me.

There were three medics at the aid station. There was one other guy on a stretcher, but nothing much was going on. The medics were mostly gabbing among themselves.

I lay there for about forty-five minutes. Nobody was paying any attention to either me or the other guy. I started to worry. What was going to happen? Was Captain Sawyer just giving me a rest? At the end of the day was he going to give me some pills and send me back on duty?

Finally I couldn't stand the suspense any longer. I had to know what was going to happen.

The next time a medic came by, I called up to him. "Say, what happens next?"

He was a tall, skinny guy. He gave me an irritated look. Having information you are seeking makes some people feel superior and they are reluctant to give out the information because then they will lose their superiority. And this medic knew who I was. He had seen me around.

"We're waiting for an ambulance," he said curtly. "When it gets here, it'll take you to a field hospital."

Things were looking better and better. Only good could come of this.

I didn't want to just disappear. I wanted to tell Jelich and Sergeant Drummond that I was leaving but I could see there was no way I could do that. Then I suddenly remembered my pistol. It was in the holster of my cartridge belt. As I have said, this was a weapon prized as a symbol of prestige and rank. Sergeant Drummond would want to pass it on to somebody else.

I waited for some medic other than the tall, skinny guy to come by. When he did, I said to him, "Will you make sure that Sergeant Drummond gets my .45?"

"Yeah," he said.

I was pretty sure I knew where I had picked up the jaundice germs. A farmer was walking across his barnyard with a pail of milk he had just taken from his cow in the barn. I was dying for the taste of fresh milk. I asked him to pour some into my canteen cup. He filled the cup. Sergeant Drummond was present and strongly advised me not to drink it, but I drank it anyway. It was foolish of me to do so, but I didn't care. What did it matter? I was facing 88s almost daily.

I thought about it. If I could turn back the clock and live through this again, and if I knew that milk was contaminated with yellow jaundice, would I drink it? No. That would not be honorable. That would be like shooting myself in the foot. But I didn't know there were health consequences in drinking the milk. I really thought there was very little risk involved. So how did I feel now, did I regret drinking it? No, I did not. Yellow jaundice makes you sick but an 88 can make you a lot sicker.

"The ambulance is here!" somebody called out.

I fully expected to be told to get up and walk to the ambulance. Instead two medics came over and picked up my stretcher.

To be carried about, how exhilarating! I felt like an emperor. Without a doubt this was the way to go from one place to another. To be carried about, to be taken care of, to be looked after, to be free of responsibilities, to be helpless, what a wonderful feeling.

One of the two medics carrying me was the tall, skinny guy. He was by my head. As he set me down in the back of the ambulance, he delivered a mean-spirited farewell.

"I've seen a lot of guys come through here with yellow jaundice," he said to me. "It's nothing. It's like a bad cold. You'll be back here in no time."

Beneath the cloak of friendly reassurance lurked the poison-tipped dagger of malevolence. He was sore because I was leaving and he wasn't and he wanted to get even, cause me to worry, diminish my euphoria. I didn't know anything about yellow jaundice. I had never heard of it. I didn't know anyone who had ever had it. For all I knew, what he was saying was right, but why did he have to tell me I'd be back in no time? Why couldn't he keep that to himself?

(I found out later that the medic was full of shit. Yellow jaundice was not nothing. It was not like a bad cold. Two guys in my yellow jaundice ward in the hospital died before our very eyes. Instead of getting stronger, they got weaker. Instead of getting less yellow, they got more yellow. A screen was thoughtfully placed around the bed of each dying man, so that they could die in privacy or so we wouldn't have to look at them. I don't know which. In my own case, it took months before I felt fit.)

The other guy on a stretcher was also carried into the ambulance. I didn't know what had happened to him but he was unconscious. They closed the doors behind us and we lay there. I had no one to talk to. But I really didn't mind because I didn't want to talk anyway. Too much was happening. I wanted to think.

The driver was in no hurry to leave. We lay there in the quiet ambulance for about ten minutes. Then he came and off we went.

We drove a long way. Then we stopped. I heard voices. The ambulance doors were opened. There was a bunch of people by the doors, hovering, bustling about, nurses, guys. This was real service. They were looking at our medical tags and whisking us out of the ambulance.

They carried us into a large, spacious tent. They settled us on cots. The tent was crowded with wounded men. Some of them had bottles of stuff overhead dripping down into their arms. The tent had lamps for illumination at night. I gathered from the concern on the nurses' faces and their constant monitoring of certain patients all through the night that some of these guys were touch-and-go. Every now and then one of them would cry out or groan. I didn't sleep well at all that night but not because of them. My mind was too disturbed.

The nurses were holding down the fort by themselves. I'm sure there were doctors around somewhere, but they were not in evidence in this tent. The nurses were busy. They worked quietly. I never heard one of them speak in a loud voice. They weren't gossiping with one another; they weren't flirting with anyone. I was very impressed.

Not long after I first arrived, a nurse came over to my cot. She was young and beautiful. She looked at my tag. She was in green fatigues. Her hair was nice and she had on lipstick. It was wonderful just to look at her.

She leaned over and spoke softly.

"How are you feeling?" she said.

"I'm fine," I said.

She smiled at me.

"Call me if you need anything."

"I will."

"I'll tell you what's going to happen. You'll be here overnight. Tomorrow we're going to put you on a C-47 and fly you to a hospital near Paris."

Wow! Paris. That was a long way from the front. The news was getting too good to believe.

This morning I had waked up, feeling rotten, expecting to relieve Groton at battalion CP in the afternoon, and tomorrow I would be flying in an airplane for the first time in my life. Things were moving awfully fast.

I had been in combat for three months, three months that seemed like three years. The war was winding down. By the time they treated my illness at that hospital and I had made my slow way back overland to rejoin my outfit, I felt the war would be over.

So, for me, the war was over today. I would live after all.

I felt like I was sitting on top of the world.

THE WAR IS THERE. It is a thing in itself. It stands apart from what came before and what came after. It is precious to me. I would not call it the central experience of my life. My marriage is. But nevertheless, there it sits, casting its shadow over everything. I cannot stop thinking about it. It was a profoundly "good" experience. But how can something so horrible be so good? I will leave that one to the philosophers.